WELCOME

The Legend Of Harley-Davidson

Now in its 106th year of production, can anyone argue against the notion that Harley-Davidson is the most famous make of motorcycle in the world? Over those 106 years other brand names have come and gone, but Harley stands, undisputedly the oldest motorcycle manufacturer that can claim uninterrupted production.

So, what you have in your hands is a celebration of the Milwaukee marvel. I've hugely enjoyed editing this very special one-off, and the writers, photographers and illustrators who have worked on it with me are some of the very best around.

A lot has been written about Harleys over the years, so it was a challenge to find something new to say. Well, in theory it should have been. In reality, I didn't have to look too far or think too long. In these 164 glossy pages, you'll find features on military Harleys, custom Harleys, racing Harleys, partying Harley owners ... as well as the most authoritative feature on Evel Knievel, the greatest Harley movie ever made, and a round-up of the best books about Harleys.

Harley ownership has grown enormously in recent years. The biggest single catalyst was undoubtedly the introduction of the Evo engine in the early Eighties, but since then things have just got better and better.

There are Harley-Davidson dealerships in locations you'd never have imagined to find them: In Moscow (utterly unthinkable in the early Eighties), in other ex-Eastern Bloc countries such as Poland and the Czech Republic, and in the Far East – Hong Kong, Singapore and even Beijing. There have even been rumours of an H-D showroom opening in Vietnam. Quite incredible. The whole world has been Harleyfied, and is all the better for it.

Not long before we went to press with this publication, Harley-Davidson announced that sales of new bikes were down significantly through 2008 (though up by 3% in Europe, interestingly). The explanation isn't that Harley ownership is shrinking; not a bit of it. In these difficult times, folks are hanging on to their bikes for longer, and are postponing buying a new model – no matter how appealing. And that 2009 range really is extensive; just look at what's on offer, from affordable Sportsters to the mighty V-Rod muscle. What on earth would those first Milwaukee pioneers make of their legacy if they could see it? Well, they'd be proud and rightly so – and, undeniably, absolutely stunned by just how far the names Harley and Davidson have travelled.

Steven Myatt, Editor

018

053

091

148

CONTENTS

030

070

100

THE LEGEND OF HARLEY-DAVIDSON

EDITORIAL & ART
Editor Steven Myatt steven@stevenmyatt.com
Art Editor Stephen Savage
Contributors Bob Clarke, Andy Hornsby, Steve Kelly, Louise Limb, Horst Rösler, Gareth Williams and Kelvin Halloran

ADVERTISING
Advertising Manager Clare Williamson

MARKETING
Marketing Manager Juliette Cooper

MANAGEMENT
Bookazine Manager Dharmesh Mistry +44 (0) 20 7907 6100
Operations Director Robin Ryan
Group Advertising Director
Julian Lloyd-Evans
Circulation Director Martin Belson
Finance Director Brett Reynolds
Group Finance Director Ian Leggett
Chief Executive James Tye
Chairman Felix Dennis

A DENNIS PUBLICATION
The "Magbook" brand is a trademark of Dennis Publishing Ltd. The Legend of Harley-Davidson is produced by Myatt Media Ltd for Dennis Publishing Ltd. All material copyright 2009.

LICENSING & REPRINTS
To license this product, please contact Winnie Liesenfeld on +44 (0) 20 7907 6134 or email:
winnie_liesenfeld@dennis.co.uk
Dennis Publishing operates an efficient commercial reprints service. For more details please call +44 (0) 20 7907 5281

1900 TO 1909

1901

William S Harley designs a 116 cc engine for use in a bicycle frame.

President McKinley assassinated. Theodore Roosevelt becomes president. Henry Ford designs, builds and races his first automobile.

1903

First Harley-Davidson motorcycle constructed – mostly hand-made with parts bought in. The 10.2 cubic inch – 167 cc – single-cylinder engine propels the bike to about 6 mph on the flat, but hills are a problem. Final transmission is by belt.

USA sponsors the Panama uprising. Wright brothers make first powered flight at Kitty Hawk. Jack London's The Call of the Wild published.

1904

A Harley makes its racing debut at Milwaukee Motorcycle Race at the State Fair Park in the September, and comes fourth. Eight Harleys are produced in 1904, with capacity raised to 24.74 cubic inches (405 cc).

1905

First adverts for Harley-Davidsons appear – in the Automotive Cycle and Trade Journal. Sixteen H-Ds are made in the year. William H Davidson, son of Bill Davidson – who will go on to join the company and become president – born.

Roosevelt re-enters The White House.

1906

Production rises to almost one a week and the company moves into a new factory. The bikes are now available in grey or black – the latter giving rise to the nickname of 'the silent gray fellow'. By now the machines are looking very smart, with all bright work nickel plated over copper. Aluminium casings are highly polished. 'Cushion Fork' front suspension introduced.

1907

William S Harley gains a degree in Mechanical Engineering from the University of Wisconsin-Madison. The company produces 150 motorcycles, and they see their first sales to police departments.

Eastern half of Oklahoma becomes Indian territory.

Triumph sells 1,000 motorcycles during the year.

1908

First Police Harley sees service in Detroit.

General Electric patents the electric toaster.

1909

The first V-twin is introduced (though first shown to the public as early as 1907) and is produced alongside the single. This 53.68 cubic inch (880 cc), 45-degree model produces 7 bhp and is capable of about 60 mph – twice the speed of the singles. Production is 450 machines in 1908, and more than doubles to 1,149 in '09.

William H Taft – a Republican from Ohio – becomes president. Oklahoma admitted to the Union. W C Handy writes Memphis Blues. Mary Pickford stars in His Duty, directed by D W Griffith. The National Association for the Advancement of Colored People is formed; black people make up 10.7% of the US population of 93,402,151.

1910 TO 1919

1910

H-D's 'bar and shield' logo introduced.

Mark Twain dies. Congress adopts the Mann Act designed to stop the transportation of women across state lines for immoral purposes.

1911

The V-twin is dropped for 1910 but re-appears, re-designed and with 49.48 ci (810 cc), for 1911. The price of the most expensive Harley – the Model 7-D – is $300.

1912

First clutch mechanism appears on Harleys (employed on the rear wheel).

All V-twins were to be the future for the company, Harley's single cylinder bikes were still more popular with their customer, and the company managed to ease 4.3 horsepower out of the 30 cubic inch 8XA single. The 8XA also featured leading-link front forks, a 'free wheel control' clutch and a seat with both internal and external springing.

The liner Titanic sinks on its inaugural trip from Britain to America with the loss of 1,502 lives. New Mexico and Arizona join the USA.

1913

The company moves into a new, five-storey building on the same site. Production for the last year before the outbreak of World War One is 16,284. Chain final drive is made available; a clutch having been offered the previous year. Racing department initiated.

The Democratic winner Woodrow Wilson inaugurated as President. Indian release the Hendee Special.

1914

Internal expanding brakes fitted for the first time. Two-speed rear hub on some models.

The National Guard fire on strikers at the Rockefeller-owned Colorado Fuel and Iron Corporation, killing 20 men, women and children; 68 more people are killed in nationwide demonstrations.

More than 3,000 employees work on the 7-mile long assembly line in Indian's one million square foot factory at Springfield, Massachusetts.

1915

Harley gearboxes expand to three gears. Full wiring harness used for the first time.

Charlie Chaplin stars in The Tramp. Sinking of the Lusitania.

1916

First edition of The Enthusiast published for Harley owners.

1917

Harley bicycles launched.

US declares war on Germany. Virgin Island annexed. Conscription introduced.

1918

Across 1917 and 1918 Harley provide more than 20,000 machines to the American military after the USA enters the conflict in support of the European allies.

First signs of the influenza epidemic which will kill millions worldwide.

1919

Flat-twin W sports bike launched with in-line motor.

The Seattle General Strike effectively shuts down the city.

In Germany, BMW start making motorcycle engines.

1920 TO 1929

1920

Making 28,189 bikes a year, Harley becomes the largest motorcycle manufacturer in the world.

Panama Canal completed. 18th Amendment passed, prohibiting alcohol. 19th Amendment gives women the vote. The first commercial radio advertisement is broadcast. The League of Nations is established. US Justice Department deports thousands of aliens in its hunt for alleged communists.

Indian launches the Scout.

1921

At Fresno, California, a Harley becomes the first ever motorcycle to win a race with an average speed of more than 100 mph.

Warren Harding sworn in as president. Albert Einstein presents his theory of relativity in New York. The lie detector is patented. Washington Disarmament Conference limits naval tonnage.

1922

An iconic number enters the Harley language as the 74 cubic inch (1,200 cc) V-twin engine is introduced. Harley riders win all eight National Championship races.

The first edition of the Readers' Digest is published.

1923

President Harding dies of an embolism after suffering ptomaine poisoning followed by pneumonia. Prohibition abandoned.

Time magazine is launched.

BMW start selling their own motorcycles, the first being the R32.

1924

Citizenship Act makes Indians citizens without altering their status as tribal members. Interior Secretary Albert B. Fall and oilmen Harry Sinclair and Edward L. Doheny are charged with conspiracy and bribery in the Teapot Dome scandal.

1925

Joe Petrali races a Harley for the first time. All Harleys adopt the 'tear drop' tank shape.

Calvin Coolidge is elected president of the USA.

1926

Single-cylinder models re-introduced. Richard Byrd makes the first flight over the North Pole.

Ducati founded in Bologna.

1927

Lindbergh flies across the Atlantic non-stop.

1928

Front brakes offered on Harleys for the first time. Twin cam engine introduced on the JD model.

Bubble gum is offered for sale for the first time.

1929

The 45 cubic inch (750 cc) Flathead motor is introduced. Front brakes now available on all models. Wall Street crashes and depression hits the American economy. Sales start to fall.

Herbert Hoover, a Republican from Iowa, inaugurated president. Six gangsters from the Bugs Moran mob and another man are gunned down in a Chicago garage in the Saint Valentine's Day massacre. The Academy of Motion Picture Arts and Sciences makes its first annual awards. First car radio in operation.

1930 TO 1939

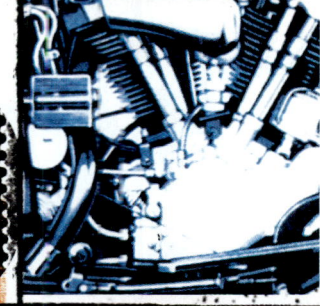

1930

William H Davidson, son of founder William, wins the Jack Pine Enduro in Michigan. That victory earns him the title of AMA National Enduro Champion for the year.

1932

The three-wheeled Servi-Car is introduced, aimed at tradesmen making local deliveries.

Prohibition is repealed. Beer flows once more!

1933

With the American economy floundering, Harley sales fall below 4,000 for the year.

A Democrat from New York, Franklin Delano Roosevelt, sworn in as president. FDR unveils The New Deal.

1934

Adolf Hitler comes to power in Germany.

1935

Single-cylinder machines are discontinued, and the 80 cubic inch Flathead motor is launched. Rikous – 'Japanese Harleys' – introduced by the Sankyo company.

Congress authorises the Works Progress Administration to put the unemployed to work on public projects, including the construction of hundreds of school buildings. Social Security Act provides retirement insurance for all Americans. Alfred Hitchcock makes The 39 Steps.

1936

The overhead valve Knucklehead motor is launched, producing 37 horsepower with 6.5:1 compression on the E model, and 40 horsepower with 7:1 compression on the EL. Four-speed transmission introduced as an option. Joe Petrali wins all thirteen AMA National Championship dirt track races on a Harley-Davidson 'peashooter'.

African-American athlete Jesse Owens wins four gold medals at the Summer Olympics in Berlin, much to Hitler's fury. Germany invades the Rhineland.

1937

All Harleys have a tank-mounted instrument panel. William A Davidson dies. WL models introduced.

President Roosevelt is heavily censored for packing the Supreme Court with his own supporters. Joe Louis defeats James J Braddock to become heavyweight boxing champion of the world.

Triumph sees huge success with its new model, the Speed Twin. Ernst Hene hits 173.88 mph on a supercharged 500 cc BMW.

1938

First Sturgis rally organised by the Jack Pine Gypsies MC in North Dakota.

United States Housing Authority established. Fair Labor Standards Act introduced.

1939

Harley-Davidson embarks on wartime production once more, starting with WLA (the 'A' standing for Army) 45 ci Flatheads.

As a result of a conference organised by Frank W Cyr, a professor at Columbia University's Teachers College all school buses are to be painted yellow. Germany invades Poland.

1940 TO 1949

1945
80 cubic inch Flathead motor dropped. A total of 90,000 WLA Harleys have been produced for the war effort. Civilian production resumes towards the end of the year.

Franklin D Roosevelt back in The White House but dies in office. Harry S Truman becomes president and attends the Yalta conference with Churchill and Stalin. American Air Force drops two nuclear bombs on Japan. Peace declared in Europe and the Far East.

Having produced 50,000 motorcycles for military use during the war, Triumph reverts to civilian production. 198,000 motorcycles registered in the US. Norton has made 100,000 bikes for the military.

1948
Panhead motor arrives (with internal oil lines, as opposed to the external lines on the Knucklehead). 74 cubic inch Flathead engine finally dropped from the range.

Bell Laboratories invent the transistor. The Berlin air-lift commences.

1941
FL series launched.

Japanese forces attack Pearl Harbour. Roosevelt initiates the Lend Lease agreement with Britain.

1942
The shaft-driven XA model, a copy of a BMW motorcycle, is ordered by the Army. Walter Davidson dies.

1943
Bill Harley dies.

1946
Race version of the 45 ci Flathead launched.

Honda Motor Company launched. Sunbeam launches the in-line twin S series.

1949
Production of WLAs resumes as America embarks on the Korean War. Production will run until 1952. Telescopic Hydra-Glide front suspension introduced. Bikes now given names rather than just initials and numbers, Hydra-Glide being the first. Harley-Davidson Riders Club of Great Britain established.

Harry S Truman sworn in again. America and the leading European countries form the North Atlantic Treaty Organisation. Russia explode a nuclear device. Communists take control in China.

Triumph release their first 650, the Thunderbird. Matchless and AJS launch their first vertical twin engines.

1944
Allied forces land in Normandy to start the invasion of Europe. The USAF starts bombing of Japan.

Having already acquired Sunbeam, BSA buys Ariel.

1947
125cc S-125 launched – and sells 10,000 in the first ten months of production. Harley buy new manufacturing premises at Capitol Drive, which was previously occupied by a company making propellers.

Marshall Plan put into force in Europe as Cold War with USSR begins. Henry Ford dies at his Dearborn estate. Jackie Robinson becomes the first black American to play major league baseball.

1950 TO 1959

1950

Arthur Davidson dies, having outlived his co-founders, but still only 69 years old.

Senator Joseph McCarthy begins his crusade against communism in the USA.

1951

Foot gear change announced for the Hydra-Glide.

The Twenty-second Amendment limits the Presidency to two terms.

Triumph buys BSA for £2.5 million.

1952

Foot-operated gear controls and hand-operated clutches introduced. The 45 cubic inch K-Series – precursor of the Sportster – introduced, with single unit engine and gearbox. First option of rear suspension; a simple swinging arm and dual coil-over shocks system. Following an attempt to gain a 40% tax advantage over imported motorcycles, Harley-Davidson is charged with operating restrictive practises. Smaller (61 cubic inch) Panhead motor deleted.

Suzuki launched.

1953

Indian motorcycles close, leaving H-D alone in the American big bike market. Model 165 replaces the S-125 (with 165 cc, naturally).

Dwight D Eisenhower becomes president. American troops partially withdrawn from South Korea as the war comes to an end.

Norton sold to AMC. Ariel launches the 1,000 cc Square 4.

1954

'54 models used as fiftieth anniversary machine rather than those made in '53. Otherwise Harley always acknowledged 1903 as the company's first year. The factory launch the Golden Anniversary KH Sports and KHK Super Sports

Kawasaki Heavy Industries begin trading.

1955

Electra-Glide launched with an electric starter (and heavier duty battery to cope with it). New cylinder heads add 10% more power to cope with the Electra-Glide's weight. The 125cc Hummer is launched, named after Dean Hummer, a Harley dealer in Omaha, Nebraska who led the field in national Harley two-stroke sales. Hot KHK street bike with 2-into-1 exhaust introduced.

Johnny Allen hits 193mph (310kph) on Bonneville Salt Flats, riding a 650cc Triumph streamliner. Yamaha Motor Company opens its doors.

1957

XL Sportster introduced.

1958

A faster Sportster – XLH with higher compression and larger valves – is launched, along with the even more rapid XLC & XLCH (Competition/California Hot) models. Plus, the XLR and XLRTT competition bikes appear, with up to 82 horsepower. The Hydra-Glide becomes the Duo-Glide, with a sprung seat and hydraulic suspension front and rear. Texan Carroll Resweber wins the first of four consecutive AMA Grand National Championship titles on Harleys.

1959

Alaska and Hawaii become states of the USA.

Triumph introduce the Bonneville. First Japanese motorcycles – Yamahas – on sale in America.

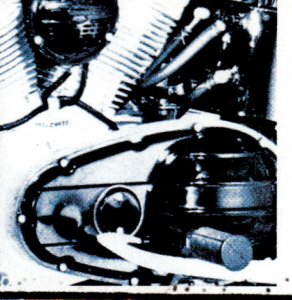

YEAR **00** **01** **02** **03** **04** **05** **06** **07**

1960

Harley buys 50% of Aeronautica Macchi's motorcycle arm and begins selling the Aermacchi 250 horizontal single in the States under the name Sprint. The Topper scooter is launched. Super-10 replaces both the Hummer and the Model 165.

Gary Powers captured by the Russians after his U-2 spy plane is shot down.

1961

John F Kennedy becomes president. Invasion of Cuba at the Bay Of Pigs. America finishes development of the first intercontinental ballistic missile. Kennedy launches the Apollo project to put a man on the moon. Alan Shepard becomes the first American in space.

Steve McQueen rides a Triumph TR6 in The Great Escape.

1962

The Ranger, a small off-road bike is introduced to use up the factory's supply of 165 cc engines from the Model 165. The Pacer replaces the Super S-10, now 175 cc. Last of the new small-capacity bikes is the Scat, with high-mounted exhaust pipe, and street-legal off-road tyres.

Cuban missile crisis. John Glenn becomes the first American to orbit the earth.

Honda make a big impact in the USA with their 'You meet the nicest people on a Honda' advertising campaign.

1963

H-D buys a glassfibre business which was previously only making boats.

John Kennedy assassinated in Dallas, Texas. Vice President Lyndon Johnson sworn in as president.

1964

Willie G Davidson, grandson of co-founder William Davidson, joins the company, working in the design facility.

1965

The Electra-Glide is launched. George Roeder sets a world record for 250cc motorcycles, hitting 177.225 mph on a Sprint. H-D becomes a public company after more than sixty years in private ownership. 125cc Bobcat launched – only in production for one year.

First demonstrations against the war in Vietnam. The Beatles tour America for the first time. Black activist Malcolm X assassinated.

1966

Harley introduces the Shovelhead engine.

1967

Electric start offered as an option on Sportsters.

1968

H-D replaces its American-made two-stroke with the 125cc Rapido made by Aermacchi.

Martin Luther King assassinated. Robert Kennedy assassinated.

Triumph and BSA introduce the 125 mph, 750cc Trident and Rocket 3. Norton launch the750 cc Commando.

1969

H-D is bought by AMF and large numbers of workers are made redundant. A strike follows. Quality falls dramatically and the Japanese importers see H-D riders moving over to their bikes in large numbers.

Richard M Nixon becomes president. Neil Armstrong becomes first man to walk on the moon. Nixon visits China. Easy Rider released, starring Peter Fonda and Dennis Hopper.

Honda introduces the 4-cylinder CB750.

1970 TO 1979

1970

Gorgeous and iconic XR-750 flat-tracker introduced, weighing just 295 lbs from its tuned 45 cubic inch Sportster motor. Cal Rayborn records 265 mph on his Harley-powered streamliner at Utah.

American forces invade Cambodia. Thirteen students shot by the National Guard at Kent State University in Ohio, four fatally.

Royal Enfield closes. BSA launches the Ariel 3 three-wheeler.

1971

FX 1200 Super Glide designed by Willie G Davidson appears in dealer showrooms. The bike has an elaborate seat unit, king 'n queen seat and red, white and blue paint. Riding a Harley, Joe Smith becomes the first drag racer to crack 9 seconds.

American Gross National Product hits $1 trillion.

1972

The 1,000 cc (61 cubic inch) XL Sportster replaces the 900 cc model. The bike costs around $2,000 depending on specification. For the first time disc brakes are offered. Alloy-engined version of the XR750 arrives.

1973

First AMF badges on Harley-Davidson motorcycles. William H Davidson resigns after clashes with the AMF board. Hand gear change dropped from big twins.

Richard Nixon sworn in as president for second term. Members of AIM seize the trading post at Wounded Knee, South Dakota. South Vietnam surrenders to North Vietnam. America withdraws from the country. Vice President Spiro T Agnew resigns. The movie Electra-Glide In Blue starring Robert Blake and Billy Green Bush released.

Norton-Villiers-Triumph formed.

1974

Harley buys out Aermacchi completely. The company moves its assembly plant to York, Pennsylvania.

Nixon steps down ahead of impeachment over the Watergate scandal. Gerald Ford sworn in. Ford pardons Nixon.

1975

Harley production hits 75,403 motorcycles.

5 million motorcycles registered in the US. Suzuki introduces the Wankel-engined RE5.

1976

Vikings 1 and 2 land on Mars. America celebrates the 200th anniversary of the declaration of independence. Jimmy Carter elected president.

1977

FXS Low Rider and FLHS tourer introduced to the line.

Alex Haley's book Roots becomes a huge TV hit.

1978

Aermacchi is sold to Cagiva. 75th anniversary models introduced, including lovely XL-1000 Sportster with jet-black paint, gold striping, gold-tinted cast wheels and 2-into-1 exhaust. First electronic ignition.

American Indian Religious Freedom Act makes native religious practices legal. Americans held hostage in Iran after the revolution which deposed the Shah.

1979

XLCR Sportster café racer launched. Fatbob introduced.

USA recognises the communist Chinese government. American Embassy in Iran occupied.

Honda introduces the 6-cylinder CBX.

1980 TO 1989

1980

FLT Tour Glide gets rubber-mounted engine. Kevlar belts replace chain drive. FXWG Wide Glide launched.

The Official Preppy Handbook published. Average cost of a new house in the USA was $68,714.00, and the average wage stands at $19,170.00. John Lennon shot dead outside his home at the Dakota Building in NYC.

1981

A group of 13 investors, including Vaughn Beals and Willie G Davidson buy H-D from AMF for $80 million.

Ronald Reagan becomes president. Stephen Spielberg releases ET. Britain defeats Argentina in a short war after Argentina invades the Falkland Islands.

1983

At the urging of Harley-Davidson a 45% import tariff is placed on foreign motorcycles, following claims that these bikes were being 'dumped' in the USA below cost. There's a new Sportster – the XR-1000 – and more than 1,000 are sold despite the high price of $6,995. The FXR now available with anti-dive front forks. Harley Owners' Group founded.

Ronald Reagan announces proposal for Star Wars defence shield. America forces invade Grenada.

John Bloor buys Triumph. BMW introduces its 4-cylinder, 1,000 cc K100. First Buell racer built.

1984

Harley release the all-new, computer-designed Evolution V-twin engine, with aluminium cylinders (but not used on all models; Shovelhead engine still in production). The motor produces 70 horsepower with a capacity of 81.8 cubic inches (1340 cc) and proves a huge boost for the company. Softail models launched, with a single line running from the headstock to the rear axle giving a retro, rigid-frame look to the bikes.

1985

Last year of the big Shovelhead V-twins.

Ronald Reagan sworn in for his second term.

1986

The Sportster version of the Evolution engine is launched in both 883 and 1200 cc sizes. The FLSTC – Heritage Softail Classic – is introduced; the apogee of retro Harley styling. H-D stock available on the market once again. H-D buys the Rambler company which makes motor homes.

The space shuttle Challenger explodes on take-off, killing all seven crew. First Martin Luther King Jnr holiday celebrated.

1987

Low seat-height Sportster Hugger launched, aimed primarily at female riders. Harley listed on the New York stock exchange.

Tom Wolfe's Bonfire Of The Vanities published, mocking the endless pursuit of wealth. Frederick Drew Gregory becomes the first black person to command a space shuttle. The Simpsons cartoon family is first seen on The Tracey Ullman show.

1988

Softail Springer released, fitted with pre-Second World War-style springer front forks. First 1200 cc Sportster. Harley launches its Travelling Museum road show.

1989

George Bush Snr sworn in as president. American troops invade Panama and arrest drug trafficker Manuel Noriega. African-American General Colin L Powell named chair of the United States Joint Chiefs of Staff. Berlin wall falls; end of communism in Europe.

First bikes produced by re-born Triumph.

1990 TO 1999

1990

Introduction of the Fat Boy re-established Harley's supremacy in the over-750 cc market.

Iraq invades and occupies Kuwait; American forces invade to drive Saddam Hussein's forces out.

Triumph moves into new factory at Hinckley in Leicestershire.

1991

Sportster gearboxes are now 5-speed rather than 4. Dyna models launched.

A huge fire in Oakland, California claims the lives of 25 people.

1992

All Harleys now come with belt final drive (just like the pioneers).

America embarks on first Gulf War after Iraqi invasion of Kuwait.

The 5,000th Triumph leaves the Hinckley factory and the company launches the 147 bhp Daytona 1200.

1993

Harley 'Ride Home' established as an annual event for the 90th anniversary. William H Davidson dies.

Bill Clinton starts first term as president. Japan overtakes the USA as largest producer of motor vehicles.

Buell build first road bikes.

1994

Dyna frame replaces the FXR for H-D conventional parallelogram-framed machines. FLHR Road King launched.

President Bill Clinton involved in property and sexual scandals.

Last Norton produced.

1995

First fuel injection system seen on the 30th Anniversary Ultra Classic. FXSTB Bad Boy launched.

Oklahoma bomb kills 160 people.

1996

1200 cc Sportsters split into Sport and Custom.

1997

Harley opens new Production Development Center. First Sportster built in Kansas City.

Bill Clinton inaugurated for second presidential term.

Triumph production passes the 50,000 point.

1998

New H-D facility in Brazil opens.

Monica Lewinsky scandal rocks the Clinton administration; the House of Representative approve two out of four motions to impeach the president. American bombers hit targets in Afghanistan and Sudan.

1999

Twin Cam 88 engine supersedes the Evo motor. Produces 80 horsepower from its 88 cubic inches (1450 cc), which makes it the largest Harley motorcycle engine to date. Ford launches the Harley-Davidson pickup truck. FXDX Dyna Sport with adjustable suspension debuted. Softail Deuce arrives in showrooms.

American and European forces in action in Kosovo. Panama gains control of the Panama Canal. 12 students are killed and 23 other wounded in the shooting at Columbine High School in Colorado.

2000 TO PRESENT DAY

2000

The 88B version of the Twin Cam engine contains counterbalancing shafts to reduce engine vibration.

Triumph re-introduces the Bonneville.

2001

The 69 cubic inches (1130 cc) Revolution engine appears on the dramatic, all-new V-Rod street bike. The engine – jointly developed with Porsche – runs right up to 9,000 rpm and produces 115 horsepower. Uniquely for a Harley engine it is water-cooled rather than air-cooled, and the V is 60 degrees rather than 45. It also has four overhead cams rather than two, and is fuel injected. XL883R launched as a tribute the XR750.

George W Bush becomes president. Islamist attack on The World Trade Center in New York City kills 2,752. American forces test Son of Star Wars shield. US forces in action in Afghanistan for the first time. Patriot Act comes into force, strengthening anti-terrorism laws.

2002

Tough-looking, Softail-framed FXSTB Night Train introduced (originally all black)

Enron fraud revealed after its bankruptcy late the previous year.

2003

American forces, supported by British and other Allied troops, invade Iraq. Saddam Hussein found hiding in a hole in the ground by US forces. Huge electricity black-out across northern and eastern states.

2004

H-D shares drop from more than $60 to less than $40 following allegations of inflated sales figures for the previous year.

2005

1250cc Screamin' Eagle variant of the Revolution engine available.

George W Bush sworn in for second term.

2006

Work starts on Harley museum. FLHX Street Glide launched – a cross between a street bike and a tourer – designed by Willie G Davidson as his perfect personal bike. Limited edition 165 horsepower 1300 cc (79 ci) VRXSE Destroyer drag bike launched. Chinese dealership announced.

Patriot Act renewed.

2007

Harley shares top $70. The Twin Cam motor expands to 110 cubic inches (1800 cc).

2008

H-D buy Italian motorcycle manufacturers MV Agusta and Cagiva. FLHTUCTG Tri Glide Ultra Classic, the first three-wheeled Harley since the Servi-Car announced, with an exclusive 103 cubic inch engine. 1250 cc engine standard across all V-Rod models. New for the year is the all-black Night Rod Special. 105th anniversary celebrated.

Barack Obama elected to the American presidency, becoming both the first black man in the post and the youngest ever.

2009

Harley-Davidson report decreased revenue, net income and earnings per share for 2008 as economic situation bites, but announce plans to ship between 74,000 and 78,000 bikes in the first quarter of the new year.

President Obama makes a prime-time TV appeal seeking support for his massive, $800 billion economic stimulus plan.

THE CAROLE NASH TIMELINE
1985 TO 2009

YEAR 00 01 02 03 04 05 06 07 08 09

1985 Carole Nash uses a £2,500 redundancy cheque to found the company at her home in the Manchester suburb of Timperley. First month turnover is £834, with Carole specialising only in classic and vintage bikes. Today the company is the UK and Ireland's biggest motorcycle insurance specialist, protecting over 300,000 classic, vintage, modern, scooter, moped, custom, trail and touring bikes.

1991 Carole Nash appears on Granada's Flying Start, a series in which fledgling North West entrepreneurs battled for honours – and a cash prize to give them that flying start. Its panel of business experts advises Carole she will never be one of the 'big boys'!

1997 Having two years earlier claimed market leadership of the classic motorcycle insurance sector, the company turns its attention to modern bikes. It follows the same 'added value' philosophy including with every modern policy extensive UK and European breakdown and recovery, motor legal protection to recover uninsured losses and foreign travel entitlement.

1999 After pleas from Irish motorcyclists Carole Nash enters Ireland, its arrival announced with Harley riding pop star Ronan Keating opening its Dublin office. John Wheeler, Chair of the Irish Motorcycle Action Group describes concludes it as 'the best thing to happen to Irish motorcycling in 25 years'. Irish bikers clearly agreed – the company is now Ireland's biggest bike specialist with an estimated 50% market share.

2002 To help curb rising claim costs and minimise premiums, Carole Nash creates a UK-wide network of approved motorcycle repairers, headed by its own £250,000 North West Service & Repair Centre. Repair costs fall by 13 percent in the first year of operation.

2003 A double triumph at the British Insurance Awards as Carole Nash is named Personal Lines Broker of the Year and takes The Training Award.

The Hairy Bikers' Hawg Haven customs were unveiled on the Carole Nash stand at the 2008 International Motorcycle & Scooter Show.

2006 The company becomes the first major bike specialist in the UK to launch a dedicated off-road policy – again in response to pleas from enthusiasts.

2007 The company breaks new ground with a "Modern Classics" policy which gives owners of bikes as young as 10-years old access to discounted classic motorcycle insurance. In a busy year it also launches Britain's Got Biking Talent, a quest to find the nation's most beautiful machine. Some 1,500 bikes are entered and nearly 45,000 votes cast. The following year 'Sick 'n' Twisted', a curly-wurly custom chrome creation built around a Harley Davidson engine and a turbo-charged Yamaha R1, is among winners.

2008 For the sixth time in seven years Carole Nash is confirmed as the UK bikers' favourite broker – thousands of RiDE magazine readers vote it Most Used Broker in the annual RiDER Power survey. At the Carole Nash International Motorcycle Show the company pulls out all the stops by unveiling Harleys created by custom kings Hawg Haven for Charley Boorman and Hairy Bikers Si King and Dave Myers - and then launching Carole Nash Construct, the UK's first live custom bike build. Over 11 days and 400 man hours, Hawg Haven create the £30,000 Carole Nash Old Skool Bobber in front of hundreds of thousands of curious bikers' eyes. Built around a Santee Rigid frame and Revtech 1450 engine, the bike is completed within minutes of the show closing.

2009 The Carole Nash Old Skool Bobber embarks on a tour of UK and Irish bike shows, kicking off in Dublin at the Carole Nash Irish Motorcycle & Scooter Show. The end of the tour will see the bobber returning to the NEC for the Carole Nash International Motorcycle & Scooter Show 2009 where it will be given away to the lucky winner of a free prize draw.

Visit **www.carolenash.com** or call **0800 988 0261**

CAROLE NASH

Words: Steven Myatt
Photos: Steve Kelly

STURGIS:
THE PARTY
NEVER ENDS

The town of Sturgis in Meade County, South Dakota is much like any other small rural town in the USA. It lies in the west of the state, not far from Wyoming. There are around 6,500 people there, living in just over 1,700 households across the town's 3.7 square miles. The population is 95% white, and according to federal government criteria, just over 10% of the total population lives below the poverty line. So far, so fairly ordinary. The good news, for guys, is that there are more women than men; the ratio is 100 girls to every 86 guys, so far as the over-18s are concerned.

The town gained city status as long ago as 1888, and it has a strong sense of its history. It's up in the hills - the Black Hills - with an average height of 3,400 feet above sea level, so the air is clear and crisp, and it's far from being a bad place to live.

There's an airport, out to the east, and the interstate forms a sort of angular crescent below the town, running from north-west to south-east. Main Street is towards the northern edge of the town, running parallel with Highway 34, one block above it. The Bear Butte national park is about five miles to the north-east; the larger Custer Park is to the south; and the vast Badlands national park is a few miles away to the south-east. So we're talking good countryside here.

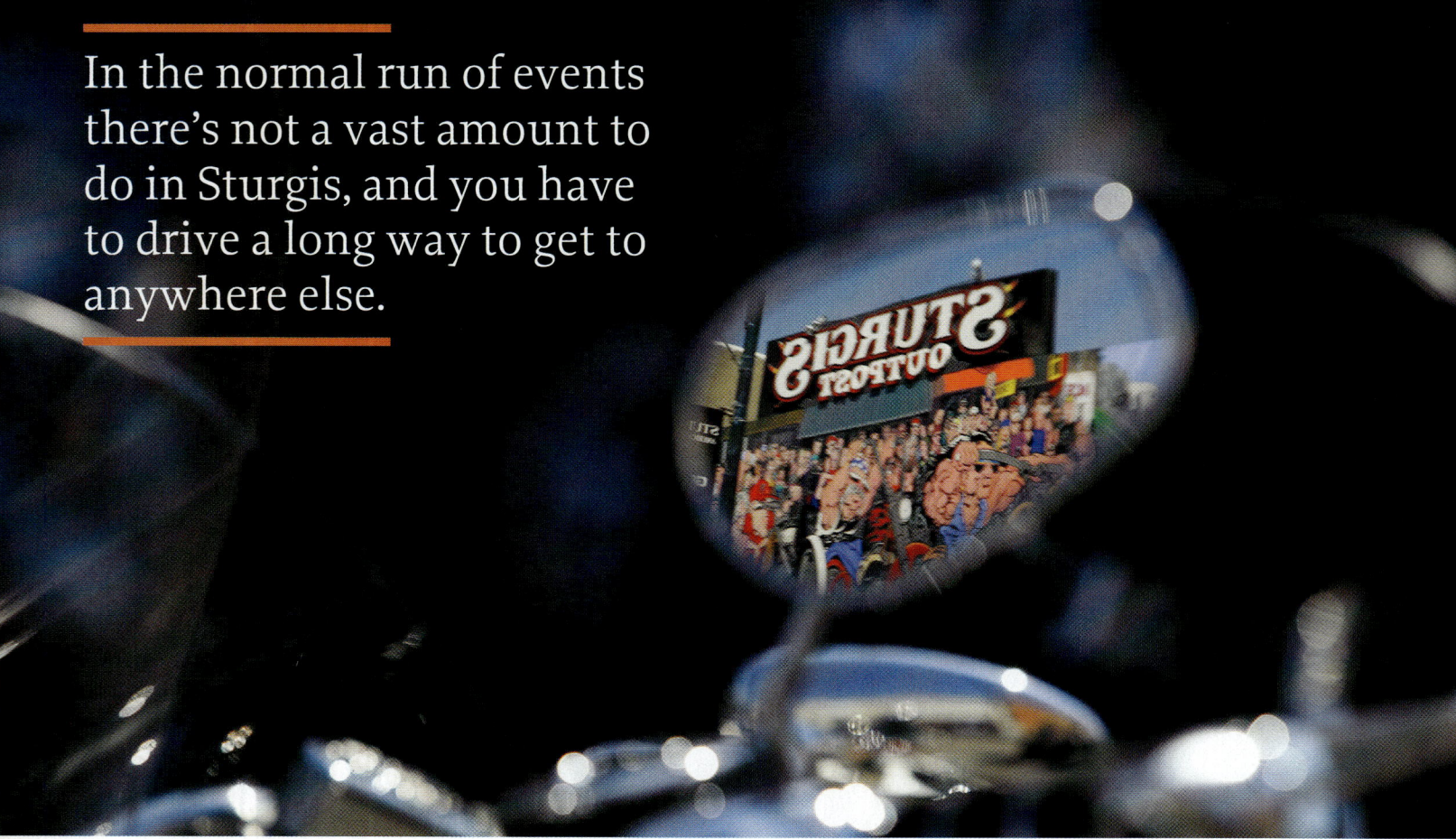

In the normal run of events there's not a vast amount to do in Sturgis, and you have to drive a long way to get to anywhere else.

In the normal run of events there's not a vast amount to do in Sturgis, and you have to drive a long way to get to anywhere else. Your best bet is to try Rapid City, off to the south, which is nearly ten times the size. Sometimes, though, the fun comes to Sturgis.

At 999 Main Street you'll find that an old church has been converted into a motorcycle museum. It opened to the public on June 1 2001, thanks to the hard work of the local people and the generosity of collectors who loaned their bikes as exhibits. If you're ever in the town then it's well worth a visit. So what? A lot of towns have museums? Well, step inside and all becomes clear.

In the late summer of 1936 the local bike club, The Jackpine Gypsies, held their first motorcycle rally. The club had only been in existence for two years, and the weekend-long rally was a touch ambitious. All over the country, bikers were doing much the same sort of thing; getting together in open spaces, organising some races, handing out trophies, having a few beers, laughing at the spills and generally having fun. The Gypsies were very far from being the first to do so, and they weren't the last. For some reason or other, though, what they did up in Sturgis had all the right ingredients; everything was just so, and over the years and decades the modest rally became bigger and bigger. Then bigger still.

The club was well-run and started to earn real money from their events. They built a clubhouse and bought the land used for the Rally (nowadays they own forty acres between junctions 30 and 32 on interstate 90).

Ten great acts who have played Sturgis

1 The Band
2 Willie Nelson
3 The Marshall Tucker Band
4 Joan Jett & The Blackhearts
5 Eric Burdon
6 Wolfman Jack
7 Robbie Krieger with Little Caesar
8 The Fabulous Thunderbirds
9 Sha Na Na
10 Steppenwolf

PERMANENT
SKULED
MONTANA

Fathead's

MISSOURI
FOXXE
SHOW-ME STATE
APR
M 1416967
08
MO

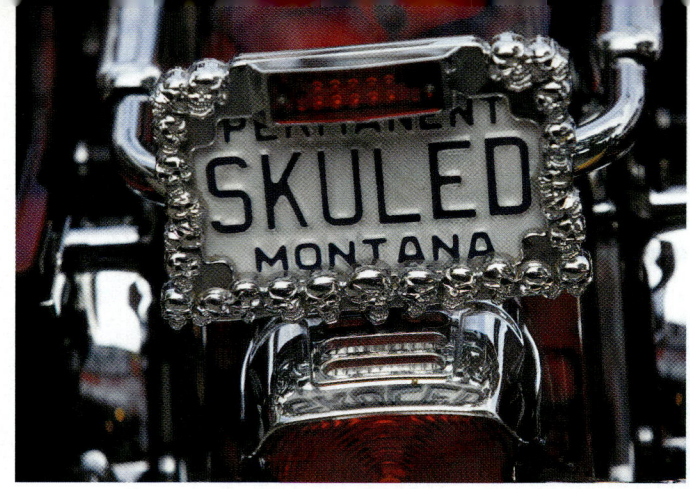

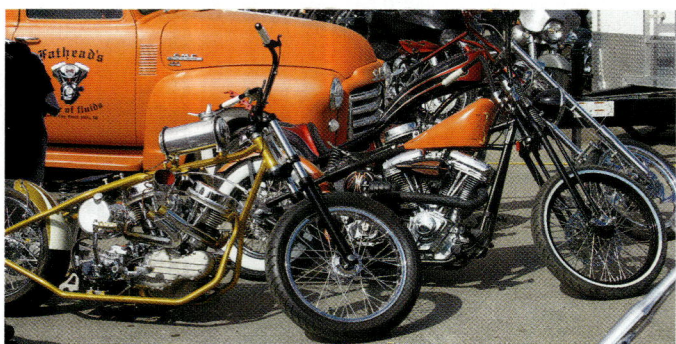

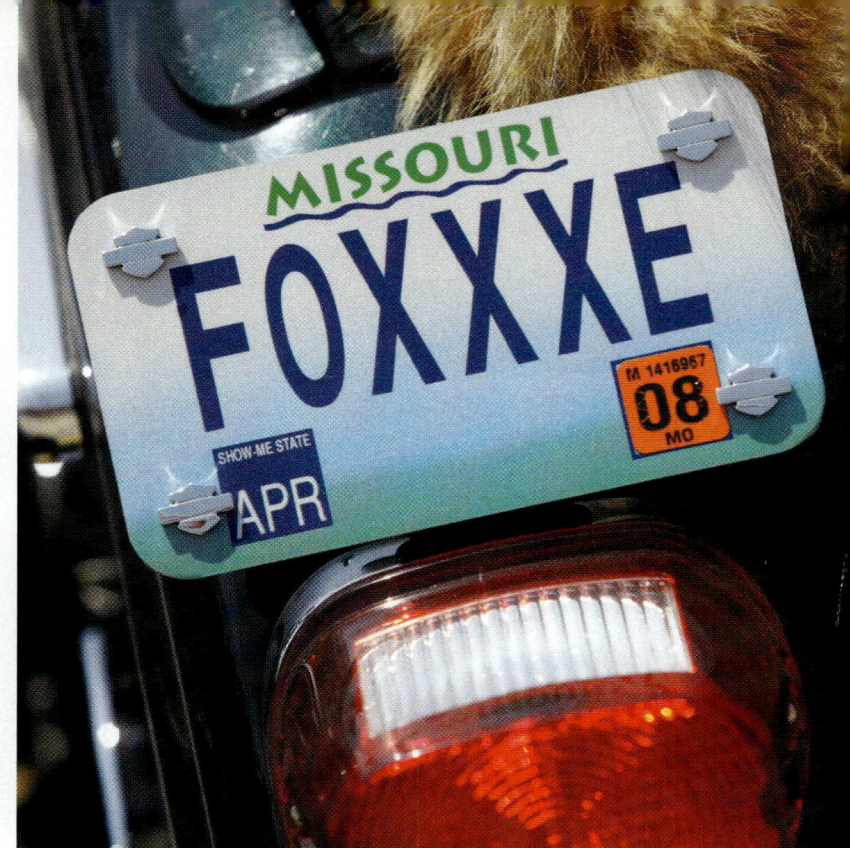

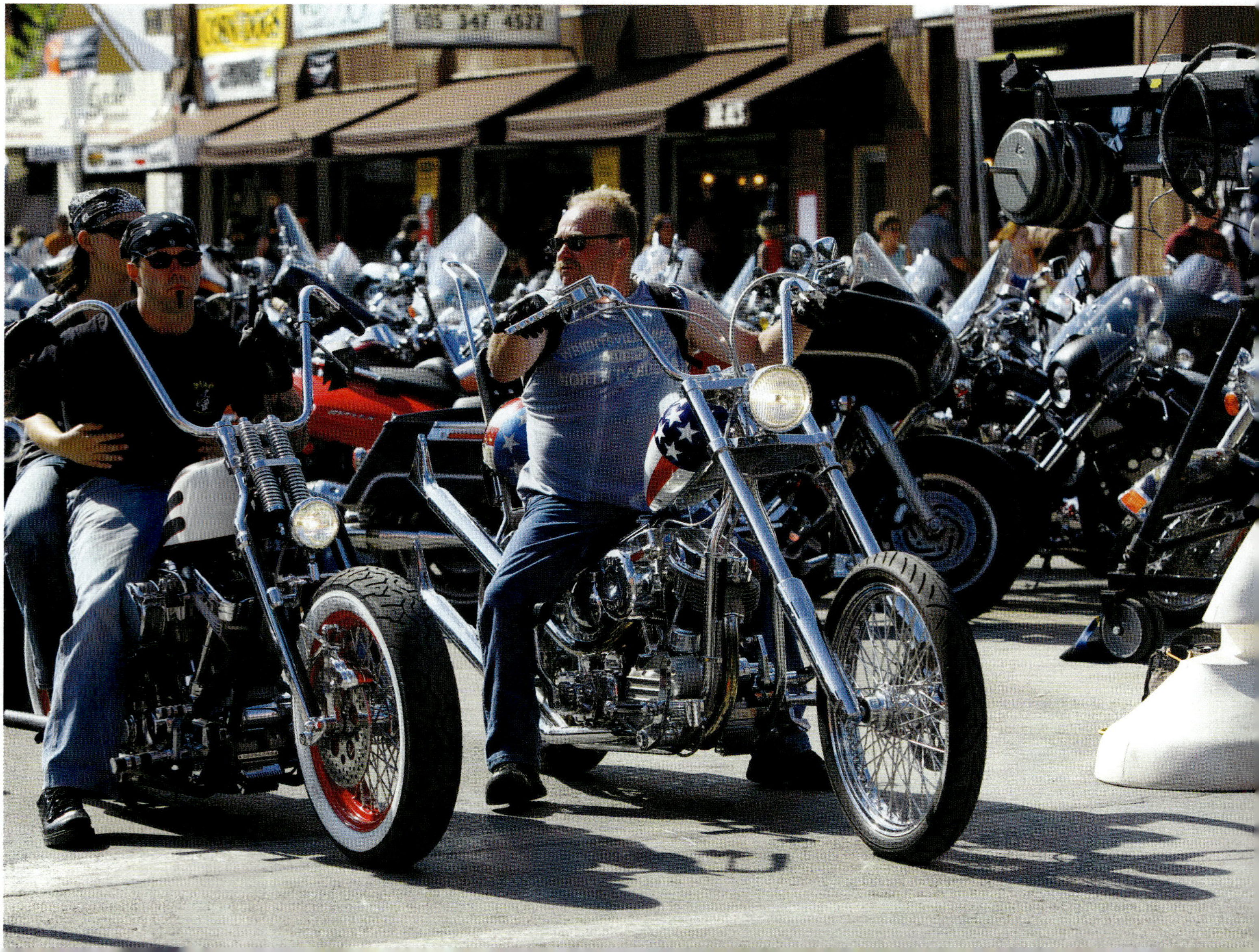
CORN DOGS
605 347 4522

Officially The Black Hills Motor Classic, it was fortunate it had a leading light in John Clarence Hoel, universally known as Pappy. He had the local Indian dealership, and had both the business experience and the enthusiasm for motorcycling to make the event a real success. The first Rally attracted 200 people, and twelve riders competed on the half-mile dirt track. Pappy said that he thought that total was sufficient reward for the effort (throughout the racing, Pappy's wife, Pearl, served free iced tea and coffee to all-comers).

Pappy had organised a big-name draw to bring in the enthusiasts; racer Johnny Spiegelhoff, known as The Milwaukee Demon. Born in 1915, Johnny was one of the biggest stars of dirt track racing. His bike was an Indian Scout, so perhaps Pappy was able to pull a few strings to get him there. Almost needless to say, Johnny won the weekend-long event.

Sturgis had been a centre for racing for some time, even before the Gypsies came along. A horse-race track was established towards the end of the nineteenth century. It stretched along Bear Butte so that spectators could watch from the higher river banks. The track was washed away during floods, so the races transferred to Main Street. The town's burghers put an end to that madness in 1910, and in 1911 a new race track was built just outside the city limits.

It was this track that was first adopted by fans of the new-fangled internal combustion engine. Car and bike races were held there, and banking was added to the corners so that higher lap speeds could be achieved. The economic crisis at the end of the Twenties brought an end to that though, but the foundation stone for years to come had definitely been laid.

The Rally – or simply 'Sturgis' – started to really grow through the ▶

Crucial Sturgis Dates

1936	The Jackpine Gypsies club formed
1937	The Gypsies join the AMA
1938	First Rally held, August 14
1942	Rally cancelled due to wartime
1961	Hillclimb and motocross introduced
1964	The Rally takes over Main Street
1965	Rally becomes a five-day event
1975	The event extends to seven days
1988	Record 118 vendors licensed by the city
1989	Founder Pappy Hoel dies aged 85
1990	Fiftieth rally celebrated
1996	New race track built
2000	Highest ever attendance; 600,000

Throughout the racing
Pappy's wife, Pearl,
served free iced tea and
coffee to all-comers

Top Ten Sturgis Facts

> August 3 to 9 2009 sees the 69th Sturgis Rally

> Just so you can programme your satellite navigation system, Sturgis is at Latitude 44° 24' 41" N, Longitude 103° 30' 52" W

> Oh yes, and the zip code is 57785

> The latest figures for the number of riders attending is the 2007 total of 461,507

> Celebrity Sturgis-goers have included Mickey Rourke, Jay Leno, the late Malcolm Forbes and Peter Fonda

> Jackpines refer to the Ponderosa pines which are common in the Black Hills

> The Ellsworth Air Force Base just north of Sturgis includes 50 Minuteman missiles in underground silos

> Fort Meade, after which the county is named, was a US Cavalry station

> By 1940 attendance at the Rally was around 800. It hovered around the 1,000 mark throughout the Fifties

> The Indian name for the Black Hills was Paha Sapa; Lakota for 'black hills'

late Eighties and the Nineties. That growth was fuelled both by the changing profile of motorcyclists, and the rise of bike-related commerce. Success breeds success. The club was soon able to donate worthwhile sums of money to local charities, and their profile in the community became high. It was realised that the visitors were bringing money into the town and spending it there, and everyone was happy. Over the years the race track became wider and gained permanent seating. Eventually a new track was built. Pappy died in 1989, aged 85. Pearl died in 2005, just a few months short of her hundredth birthday.

The local police took a relaxed view of the event, in the main, and tended to let things sort themselves out, so the Rally gained a reputation for being a good place to be. There was trouble through the late Seventies and early Eighties, it must be said, but nothing that made national headlines and cursed the event with a bad reputation. The hassles faded away as quickly as they had arisen.

Elements of the rally became sponsored, larger numbers of traders started to come for the event. Nowadays, as the figures demonstrate, Sturgis is enormous. Numbers have levelled out just below half a million – in a town with a regular population of 6,500, remember – and it has become an institution; not just within motorcycling, but a national, American institution. And if you've never been, then make yourself a promise. This is the year to get over there. Hey, you deserve a bit of a trip, and both Aerosmith and George Thorogood & The Destroyers are playing there this year!

SM

HARLEYS AT WAR

Words & photos: Steven Myatt
Archive photos: Bob Clarke, Corbis

Warfare has always been good for industry, whether it was – as time has gone on – the manufacture of bows and arrows, cannonballs, muskets or machine guns. As well as the arms themselves, military forces need a hundred thousand other things, be they blankets and toothbrushes or ballpoint pens and rolls of barbed wire. Throughout the twentieth century, armies have also demanded motorcycles; from the very earliest day of the powered bicycle, military planners have understood their usefulness. They started off being used by despatch riders to carry messages and went on to be used as weapons platforms and ambulances.

In 1899, fourteen years after Karl Benz had produced his first, practical motor car, internal combustion-engined vehicles were in use with the German army. The first Wehrmacht trucks were made by Daimler, and by 1904 they were joined by what were almost certainly the first motorcycles in military use. For the Kaisermanovern of 1904, the German authorities bought NSU's 375 cc, 2.75 horsepower singles ... and Triumph's 489 cc, 4.25 horsepower machine. It would be fascinating to know for sure whether the German or the British bike actually went into service first, but history doesn't relate precisely.

Although the German military got motorbikes into service first, the British were ahead of them in terms of development. Well, sort of. As early as 1899, the Simms-Vickers Motor Scout was launched – essentially a four-wheeled bicycle with a Maxim gun mounted between the back wheels. That was followed three years later by the larger Motor War Car, but the War Office saw no merit in the concept and ordered neither.

In 1906, the British Army acquired motorcycles from A W Wall, a company first based in Guildford in Surrey, and then in Birmingham – and financed by the author of the Sherlock Holmes stories, Sir Arthur Conan Doyle.

The European powers were in no doubt that war was coming, and the British forces increased their military funding and purchasing accordingly. As well as defending their homeland, the British Empire covered around a quarter of the land surface of the globe, and as this would be a show-down between imperial powers, all corners of the Empire had to be defended to a greater or lesser degree. The British Army bought motorcycles from BSA (who of course made firearms by way of their core business), Clyno, Douglas, P&M, Rudge Whitworth,

Left: The American Army's first use of motorcycles was during their expedition against Pancho Villa during the Mexican wars. This is a field hospital for those early bikes.
Above: Away from the front, for now at least, a First World War officer goes for a spin on his Harley.

far larger numbers were ordered by an Army expecting the fighting to go on beyond November 1918, and many orders were later cancelled. The bike used was the 987 cc V-twin, with inlet-over-exhaust valves and a single Wheeler & Schebler carb. Military spec included acetylene lighting, a rear rack, spare wheel, and a horn. All were painted in military green, and many of the bikes were fitted with sidecars (at first just bolted to the bike's frame, and later with gearing).

As well as being used solo for any number of purposes – but most frequently for despatch riding – bikes equipped with sidecars were used, simply, for moving personnel around, and for many other duties. Sidecars might have carrier pigeons in them, or be specially adapted gun carriages. William S Harley designed a sidecar which could be fitted with a Colt-Browning Model 1904, a Browning machine gun or a British Lewis machine gun. The gunner had a small folding steel screen to give him some protection from anyone who presumed to fire back. The rider, on the other hand, just made a large and vulnerable target. Bill Harley's design was designated the 16-GC, and there was a companion model, the 16-SC, which carried a stretcher – presumably for the rider who had caught the return fire. The stretcher was positioned high up, level with the saddle, and it's a fair bet that if the bullet hadn't killed you then the journey to the field hospital well might.

A curious, later military sidecar was a low steel box about four feet wide, divided into sixteen square-section compartments in two rows. This was for carrying medium-calibre ammunition to field artillery. Heaven only knows what the weight did to the bike's handling. A post-war report praised both the Harleys and the Indians, saying that they had adapted well to the duties demanded of them.

Unlike Indian, Harley-Davidson hadn't turned its factory over to military production exclusively during the war. During 1918, they had supplied just over 8,000 bikes for domestic government use (such as police forces and the postal service), and a very healthy number to the civilian market.

Anticipating increased demand for their bikes after the war, Harley borrowed heavily and increased production. For most of the Twenties their strategy was proved right, with good home sales and ever-broadening export sales.

By the early Twenties the Army were using ◗

Scott, Sunbeam and Triumph. This disparity of supply presented considerable problems regarding standardisation, but it was important to spread the war work between as many suppliers as possible.

By 1914, Germany was also well prepared for war; three quarters of the total of 64,000 motor vehicles in the country were in military service. This figure included a considerable number of motorcycles – mostly provided by NSU – which by then had advanced a long way from its origins as a powered push bike.

After staying aside from the conflict for two and a half years, the USA entered World War One on April 6 1917 – at a time when the Army was equipped with Excelsiors, Indians, Harleys and small-capacity Cleveland lightweights.

H-D's first military contract wasn't for its own government but for the Japanese Imperial Army – ironically, in the light of subsequent events – who ordered a consignment of single-cylinder X-8-A machines in 1912. Four years later the US military procurement officials ordered an initial dozen Model 16-Js, some with sidecars. These were for use in the Mexican War and were followed very quickly by another six machines. At this point there were no differences between civilian bikes and those supplied to the military, except for the colour – drab green instead of grey.

Records vary from reference to reference, but it does seem that between 12,000 and 18,000 Harleys were supplied up to the end of hostilities (in 1917 the company made 18,522 bikes in total, and 27,608 the following year). The statistics can be confusing because the FS and LUS models, and the Model JD with its 74 cubic inch engine was in service by 1924. Across the Twenties and Thirties, Harleys were used by many other military forces, including the Germans and the Chinese. There is an account of one being used during the Spanish Civil War, but only to power a stationary generator.

The Swedish army bought just one Harley, in 1932, and built a fully armoured three-wheel tank out of it, with gun mounts inside for firing a machine gun forwards, and a tripod that could be bolted to the front of the plating so that aircraft could be fired at. It was a terrific thing, which looked a little – just a little – like a stealth combo. I must build myself a re-creation of it when I've got some time on my hands.

Within the military, the use of motorcycles was not popular. Several critical memos were written concerning the high level of injuries due

There is an account of one Harley being used during the Spanish Civil War, but only to power a stationary generator.

to accidents, and an influential faction felt that water-cooled cars would also score over air-cooled bikes. The procurers were urged to look for what were then described as 'cross-country cars' instead of bikes, which they felt would be better in more rugged conditions. The numbers of bikes used during the Second World War served to contradict these opinions.

Leading up to the war, the Germans had been buying a huge range of bikes from BMW, as well as from DKW, NSU, Victoria, Zundapp ... and yes, Triumph. The British had also been using Triumphs, and by the Thirties – to a larger degree – BSAs. When war was declared, the British War Office bought everything that Triumph had, but soon rationalised their requirements to the single-cylinder 350. BSA was soon manufacturing 1,000 bikes a week, for many other Allied forces as well as the British. In all, BSA would provide about a third of the 425,000 bikes supplied to British troops from British factories. The others included Royal Enfield, Norton, Velocette, James, Excelsior (not the American company) and Matchless.

When America entered the war in 1941, the company was producing bikes with both the Flathead and Knucklehead motors. The Army wanted the simpler 45 cubic inch WLA Flathead, and in all was supplied more than 60,000 of them. They were solidly built, reliable, and easy to mend if they did go wrong. With their hefty torque they hauled well and had no trouble pulling a sidecar. With a top speed approaching 65 mph and a dry weight of 535 lbs, they performed a broad range of duties. The Army's procurement officers had insisted that when bikes were used for slow-running duties, such as escort work, there must be no danger of the engines over-heating. To achieve this, the factory dropped the compression to 5:1 and started using aluminium heads.

One criticism of the WLA though was its limited ground clearance. At just four inches it didn't make the bike useful over really tough terrain.

Above: Harley-Davidson has never been slow with its marketing, and they were only too happy to tell the public about their role in the war effort.
Right: 'Randy was starting to worry that the enemy might surround him ...' Actually it's Canadian officer Major J B Joly briefing WLC-mounted despatch riders in 1943.

Above all though, the bike was famously tough. In training, motorcycle-riding soldiers were taught to lay the bike down once the enemy was encountered and fire, prone, from behind it – a bit like cowboys and indians in the old movies, shooting from behind fallen horses ...

In what turned out to be another long-term irony, a large number of Flatheads were sent to the Red Army in the USSR after Hitler's forces invaded Russia in June 1941. These were predominantly the standard WLA model, though a special WSR was created but never used. Large numbers of these bikes fell into civilian hands after the war and were put to all sorts of uses by ordinary riders. As late as the 1980s many were still in use, though ingenuity and local engineering expertise had be used to replace broken parts. They also kept running despite the low octane rationing of Soviet fuel.

Harley supplied a much smaller number of ELA models (A for Army, as, also in WLA), powered by the 987 cc Knucklehead engine. Both heavier and slower, they were supplied as bike and sidecar with an all-up weight of 850 lbs. Harley's UA model (with the larger-capacity, dry sump Flathead engine of either 74 or 80 ci) was supplied in small models to various armies; one of the largest consignments was to the British forces in their colony of South Africa. Motorcycles played a vital role for the British in South Africa, where they suited the terrain perfectly, and ▶

MT GESTURES

If it didn't have Harley-Davidson written on the side you wouldn't believe it, would you? But that is indeed what it is – a Harley-Davidson MT350. It started out as a British-made machine, the MT500 made by Armstrong. Between 1993 and 2000 around 1,700 were made for supply to the British Army, who used them all over the world. H-D bought the rights to manufacture the bike and dropped the capacity to 350 cc from 500 cc. They were offered for sale to the public through the normal Harley dealerships, but it was primarily for supply to the American military. It featured an oil-in-frame chassis and the engines were bought in from the Austrian manufacturer Rotax. What had been the 350 was also given an electric start and disc brakes. The front-mounted panniers replaced the Armstrong rear-mounted ones. The big box on the right-hand side at the back is a gun case. And wouldn't it be fun to turn up at a H.O.G. rally on one of these?

considerable numbers were used – both Harleys and British machines.

A single civilian-spec U Model fitted with a Model LE sidecar is known to have been equipped with a water-cooled Browning machine gun and a steel shield. The idea didn't go any further.

One Harley that never made a huge impact on the war effort was the flat-twin XA. Based on the design used by the Germans for their BMW and Zundapp machines, the XA was designed for desert use. It was very unlike the rest of the H-D range, and one of the intentions was to improve cooling by having both cylinders in the air stream. The motor

In all Harley-Davidson supplied 88,000 bikes during its involvement in World War Two.

produced around 23 horsepower at 4,600 revs, and the cylinder heads ran 100 degrees (Fahrenheit) cooler than the V-twins.

Like its German antecedents it had shaft drive, and it was also curious in having no vertical centre tubing to the frame. Although Harley built 1,000 flat-twin XAs during WW2, none saw overseas service. The problem was, the military preferred the four-wheeled and more sure-footed Jeep.

Harley tried other uses for the engine, including a collaboration with Willys (manufacturer of the Jeep) to build an XA-powered lightweight four-wheeler with the motor bored out to 49 cubic inches (802 cc). This WAC (standing for Willys Air-Cooled) was designed to be used by airborne forces and parachuted in the battle field. There was a subsequent prototype, the WAC-3, but nothing came of either of the projects.

Harley tried out a couple of three-wheeled prototypes in the early Forties. One, the Model TA, was Knucklehead-powered and had a short

bench seat over small-diameter rear wheels. Then a Servi-Car was equipped with General Electric radio equipment – and the same set-up was tried in a combo. Harley also tried out a WLA trike, with the rear wheels set closely together and a large steel rack stretched above them. None of these was as appealing to the military as the Jeep, though.

The Jeep was a serious rival for all the military motorcycles. It had a greater carrying capacity, didn't fall over, and was cheap to buy and rugged in use. It was also considered safer, but in fact the number of servicemen killed or injured in accidents involving Jeeps was horrendous. In the days before seat belts or crumple steering wheel columns, the most terrible chest injuries were incurred by drivers being impaled on the steering column.

After the war, the American military held on to a number of Harleys for general use and, particularly, for use by the Military Police, but a large number were sold off. This wasn't as easy an operation as you might think. The government didn't want to damage the motorcycle industry at home, or the dealership network. The records show that 15,000 WLAs were sold for $450 each (which was comparable with Harley's domestic civilian price for the bike), and a large number of XAs for the surprisingly higher price of $500. Some of these were used, re-imported machines, but many were brand new and a lot were still in their original crates. Three British dealers – Fred Warr, Pride & Clarke and Marble Arch Motors – converted ex-American Army WLAs to civilian spec and sold to the public.

There have always been rumours of large numbers of Harleys and other makes of bike (and lots of other stuff too) being buried in large numbers in Europe, or dumped in lakes. The Army never wanted to confirm these reports of course, for fear of being seen to be wasteful, but it does seem to have been the case. War is hugely wasteful, and as we've seen, the American government didn't want too many ex-military bikes back on native shores. Also, at the end of the war, the priority was to get troops home, not equipment.

In all, Harley-Davidson supplied 88,000 bikes during its involvement in World War Two, which is an impressive total. Many of that number did come into civilian hands after the war and went on to give cheap, accessible pleasure to a generation of bikers.

In 1948, the Army did test a possible military version of the 125 cc Model S, which Harley had just launched. Based on a DKW design, it

became the BSA Bantam in Britain, but the American military took the little Harley no further - opting instead for the equivalent Indian model.

Although they had sold off so many Harleys immediately after the war, the Army did continue buying big twins from Harley in subsequent years. Harley supplied the last Servi-Cars to the Army in 1950, and from its introduction, supplied Sportsters until 1963. Some of these were for the Navy's shore patrols, and some for the Military Police.

A post-war report praised both the Harleys and the Indians, saying that they had adapted well to the duties demanded of them.

The American forces had no use for bikes in either Korea or Vietnam, and the relationship between the military and H-D ended. When the Army started buying bikes again in the mid-Seventies, they weren't from Milwaukee, and the days of V-twin Harleys burbling across battlefields was gone forever.

Top: This is a real rarity; a TA Model Knucklehead trike as supplied to the military – albeit very briefly.
Above: The XA was based on a German design but never saw service.

MILITARY BIKES: THE ALTERNATIVES

Harley certainly didn't have it all their own way so far as supplying bikes to the military was concerned. Indian was a serious rival for many years, but there were other, lesser-known brands in contention too.

It seems likely that the first motorcycles purchased by the US Army were single-cylinder 500 cc Indians (the company being known at the time as Hendee Manufacturing, the name being changed to Indian in 1912) at the end of the first decade of the century. The first records show that US Marines were using these machines on peace-keeping duties in Haiti in 1916. The following year, also in Central America, the Marines rode 1,000 cc V-twin Indian Powerpluses - which were capable of a true 60mph - while serving in the Dominican Republic, fighting native guerrillas (by then America had occupied both countries, and stayed there until public opinion at home turned against this in the Twenties). Indian bikes were also sent into Mexico in 1916, while the Army was in pursuit of Pancho Villa. Motorcycles were bought for military use from Excelsior as well. The majority of these were the attractive, narrow-V 974 cc model.

With the USA's entry into the First World War all three companies – Excelsior, Indian and Harley – saw an opportunity to greatly increase their sales to the military. Indian, indeed, virtually abandoned its domestic, civilian market so that it could effectively bid for as many military sales as possible. They suggested that the government might like to order what was then the equivalent of their yearly production, 20,000 bikes, at prices ranging from $187.50 for a solo and $237 for a combo. By the end of the war, Excelsior had supplied 2,600 bikes, as opposed to Harley's total of 14,606 (though well over 26,000 had actually been ordered) and 14,300 sidecars. Indian had done best of the three though, having delivered more than 18,000 bikes and nearly 17,000 sidecars (though, again, far more were ordered – almost 40,000). All three models were 1,000 cc V-twins.

Motorcycle production of all kinds was badly hit by the hard times which came with the early Thirties. In 1933, fewer than 7,400 bikes were manufactured in the whole of the USA. Needless to say, although bikes had proved their worth in war, the military weren't ▶

spending money. That was to change early in the next decade though.

Henderson/Excelsior produced some terrific motorcycles after World War One, and – deservedly – they sold well. In 1922, the San Diego police set up a competition between Henderson and Harley to see which bike was the quicker, and the Chicago company beat H-D hollow.

Although the USA didn't enter the Second World War until December 1941, President Roosevelt put American forces on a state of readiness in the summer of 1939. Both Harley and Indian were to supply huge numbers of bikes to the American military (and other armed forces), but a number of other manufacturers did get a look-in too.

J Paul Treen was the Harley-Davidson dealer in Baton Rouge, Louisiana in the Thirties, and he decided that what the motorcycling world needed was a very cheap, small-capacity motorcycle. He created the Simplex company and starting producing the 4 bhp Servi-Cycle – a very basic machine, rather like the small-engined, Villiers-powered British bikes of the time. Like those manufacturers, Treen's operation never bothered making its own motors and simply bought them in. The Servi-Cycle was in production until 1960, but which time Simplex were also making scooters, go karts, and lawn mowers.

The American Army bought more than 650 of the specially produced Military-specification G models, which were designated the G-A-1. They weighed just 165 lbs and could just touch 30 mph. They had a left-hand throttle (as some Indians did) so that a soldier – presumably right handed – could ride and fire a gun at the same time.

The G-A-1 was fitted with steel rings to which a parachute could be attached so that they could be dropped into action. The better known bike in this role, though, was the Cushman. The company – whose core business was manufacturing golf buggies – produced the 244 cc Husky-engined 53 Autoglide to the military in '44 and '45. The Cushman company had been in existence since 1903, and started making bikes in 1936. They made their last bike in '65.

Capable of around 40 mph, the Autoglide's engine was mounted beneath and behind the large leather saddle. There was a flat steel step-through area for the rider's feet, and the whole thing sat on 6-inch wheels. They were heavier than the Simplex, at 255 lbs, but were sturdier – and very simply constructed. The Army bought 4,734 of them in total.

Despite the decision to stop making bikes, Excelsior did produce the 98 cc Welbike in considerable numbers – just under 4,000 in fact – for military use. Also designed to be parachuted into action alongside the troops, the Welbike was different in that the seat dropped down and the bars folded back, and it was packed into a drop cylinder. Assuming it had landed safely, the soldier unclipped the cylinder, pulled the bike out and rode off to battle.

The statistics for the number of Indians supplied during the Second World War are, unsurprisingly, rather more impressive. In all more than 35,000 of the 741 models were made, and they saw service in many different parts of the world, and with the armies of several countries. The Springfield, Massachusetts-based company's contribution to the war effort also included the 841, the 340 and the 640.

The 741B employed a 30.50 ci (500 cc) V-twin-engine and was derived from what had been the Junior Scout in civilian life. The 640 was similar but had the larger, 45 ci, 750 cc capacity. These bikes were solid workhorses; not fast – and not hugely comfortable, by all reports – but they were rugged and dependable.

The 340B had been the marque's flagship, the Chief, all 74 ci (1,200 cc) of it. It was rather plainer in military guise, supplied without its extravagant mudguards and its acres of chrome. Around 5,000 were in operation during the war.

The US government also ordered the 841 model, which was designed for desert use. It had a 744 cc, 90-degree V engine, but the cylinders stuck out to left and right, instead of running for and aft – for better cooling in hot conditions. Apart from the configuration of the motor, it looked like any other big twin of the period. The reasoning behind the bike's conception was faulty though, and they were rarely used in desert conditions. In fact they were rarely used at all. After just over 1,000 had been made the order was cancelled, and the majority of those that had been built were stored until the war ended.

SIXTY FIVE YEARS ON...

Ray Wilcox is chairman and secretary of the North Staffordshire area of the Military Vehicle Trust, and this is his WLC. Oh yes, and that's his Jeep in the background too. He restored it to Military Police spec 'because it appealed to me', and to go with the Jeep. The Jeep, by the way, dates from around 1958 and is a Hodgkiss re-build. It has a new body over wartime running gear.

Ray bought the bike about seven years ago 'on the Belgian/German border'. It's a WLC so was probably used by the Canadian army, though the RAF did have a good number too. Unfortunately you can't find out more. As Ray says, in the Sixties the British Ministry of Defence destroyed all their wartime records. Before then you could use the bike's service number to trace its history; sadly you can no longer do so.

Apparently the senior ranks tried to discourage riders from personalising their bikes by giving them names and painting pictures on them, but the lower ranks persisted and it was very common among the Americans and Canadians. It was aircraft nose art transferred to Harley petrol tanks and, it's likely that it helped the military riders form a bond with their own machines – doubtless a good thing.

The bike was in pretty good condition when Ray found it, but it required some finishing. The siren – which is spring-mounted ▸

and operates on the rear tyre thanks to a heel-operated lever – was missing, but one was found at an auto-jumble for £120 and was snapped up. The parts aren't hard to find; as Ray says, 'there was so much stuff made, and as well as everything that went into service there was a lot of reserve stock. You can always find the parts for a WL in western European countries, plus there's a very good network of reproduction parts. In most cases the new stuff is alright. And of course we can always find what we need through the Trust.'

Steve Clarke, Ray's right-hand man, also owns a WL and he says, 'they are antiquated to ride, but you do get used to them. I'd never been on one of these before I bought mine. It was in Essex and I rode it nearly 200 miles home – through London in the rush hour. No hand clutch on mine either. It took years off my life.'

'There are far more ex-military bikes, and Harleys in particular, still being ridden than you'd think', Ray says. 'There are a lot in the MVT but we keep coming across so many that we don't know about. It's impossible to say how many exactly are still on the roads, but it's a lot, considering.' **SM**

A PROUD LINE-UP

Words: Andy Hornsby:
American-V.com

THE VERY GREATEST HARLEY ENGINES

They all have their fans; some think that **Triumph** parallel twins are the most beautiful thing imaginable, and speaking for myself, I'd have the Norton Commando motor on the list too. Fans of Italian motorcycles would argue for Ducati engines or – and yes, they've got a point – the mighty Benelli Six. There aren't that many Japanese motorcycle engines that could honestly be called beautiful, are there? No. The original Honda 750 OHC lump, maybe? The so-big-it's-scary CBX six-pot? The Kawasaki 1,000 cc motor from the Seventies, the one with the H-shaped cam cover? Hmmm, dunno. When it comes to Harley-Davidson engines though, things are different. Among the V-twins, show me an ugly Harley engine. Thought not, there aren't any. I know all that aesthetic stuff about 'form following function', but how come they just look so damn good? They're designed to do a job, not to look like works of art. Is it just a happy accident? Whatever, here's a close look at our absolute favourites. Every one lovely enough to go in an art gallery, too.

KNUCKLE HEAD
1936-47

E-Series: 1936-47
989 cc / 60.53 ci (nominally 1000 cc / 61 ci)
Bore & Stroke: 3 5/16 x 3 1/2

F-Series: 1941-47
1,207cc / 73.66ci (nominally 1200 cc / 74 ci)
Bore and stroke: 3 7/16 x 3 31/32

The Motor Company's 1936 EL is often referred to as the origin of the modern Harley-Davidson V-twin, and not without good reason. It brought with it the twin fat-bob tanks, simplified instrumentation that separated it from motorcycling's pioneer days, and introduced the single camshaft design that saw service right up until the 1999 dawn of the Twin Cam.

It is frequently picked out as the landmark model by virtue of its overhead valves, but they were almost secondary compared to the other main evolution that would roll-over onto the rest of the range in the following year: a full re-circulating oil system. Previously the oil pump had purely delivered oil to the motor, which had either burned or dripped away onto dust roads, rather than being returned to the oil tank.

Its cast iron cylinder heads were topped off by aluminium castings with an almost sculpted quality about them, which, when combined with the over-sized hexagonal bolts that marked the end of each valve's rocker shafts, were reckoned to resemble the knuckles of a clenched fist. Thus the Knucklehead was born, although it's said that the expression wasn't coined until the arrival of the next generation of the motor, the Panhead. Until then it was the 61 OHV.

The replacement for the old 'inlet-over-exhaust' (or F-head) J-series, the sporty 61 cubic inch (1000cc) E ran alongside Harley's stolid touring side-valves – including the iconic W-series, the 45, as well as the U-series 74-inch and 80-inch 'Big Twin' side-valves – which it predated by a year. As flat tankers with total loss oil-systems, they had been the R and the V when the E came out.

A bored and stroked version of the E was launched in 1941 – nearly half an inch longer in the stroke and an eighth of an inch across the bore – taking it up to 74 cubic inches (1,200cc), which ran alongside the 61-inch E and was called the F-series, which still identifies what we now call a Big Twin.

PANHEAD
1948-65

The new motor for 1948, labelled the Panhead for its smooth rocker covers, built on the phenomenal success of the 61 OHV model; an ongoing success which spelt the end of the line for the Big Twin side-valves in 1948. The new motor wasn't just more sporty, it proved to be reliable as a touring mount, allowing Harley-Davidson to rationalise their range. It also left Big Twin orphaned as an expression, but that would soon be applied as a generic term to the whole F-series.

It retained the two model designations and capacities until the smaller motor was dropped in 1953, but it was in the right place at the right time to be at the heart of three landmark models. These were the 1949 Hydra Glide (so-called for its hydraulically damped telescopic front forks), the 1958 Duo Glide (with its matching hydraulically damped rear suspension), and the 1965 Electra Glide (with its electric start and cast aluminium primary chain case).

The Panhead did away with the Knucklehead's complicated multiple rocker covers and potential for oil leaks at their jointing faces and the rocker shaft's nut, concealing the entire valve mechanism for each cylinder beneath a single cast aluminium cover sealed by a single thick gasket. It also used aluminium castings for the cylinder heads – for its greater heat-dissipation properties – and combined that with silver-painted cast iron barrels to create a much more modern-looking motor. It also featured hydraulic lifters in the valve train, which didn't need constant adjustment. Combined with more sophisticated quietening ramps on the camshafts, this led to a mechanically quieter motor.

Even in its launch year, complete with Springer forks, high-mounted headlamp and fishtail silencer, it made the Knucklehead look dated, and as it progressed through to the 1960 aluminium headlamp nacelle, Panhead-equipped models just got more modern. In those three evolutions, you can see the FL Springer Softail, the Heritage Softail and the Road King. The Panhead is also often seen as the dawn of custom Harley-Davidsons too – not least because Captain America and Billy burst onto the cinema screen on Panheads.

It's little surprise then that the Panhead holds so special a place in Harley fans' hearts.

E-Series: 1948-52
Capacity: 989 cc / 60.53 ci (nominally 1000 cc / 61 ci)
Bore x Stroke: 3 5/16 x 3 1/2

F-Series: 1948-65
Capacity: 1,207 cc / 73.66 ci (nominally 1200 cc / 74 ci)
Bore x stroke: 3 7/16 x 3 31/32

K & X SERIES
1952-DATE

As if to confirm the technical marvel that was the 1936 61 OHV, you don't have to look any further than Harley-Davidson's smaller twins.

The flat tank 1936 model R became the 1937 W with the re-circulating oil system and cycle part upgrades introduced with the Knucklehead. Quite apart from liberating Europe in the hands of the Americans, Canadians, some Brits and even the Russians, it continued to feature in Harley-Davidson's production schedules until 1951. It was finally replaced by the all-new K-Series.

The K featured hydraulic suspension at both ends, and a set of crankcases that held both the engine and the transmission in separate sections, linked by the inner primary drive. This engine was designed for sporting models, to compete with the British twins that were making an impression among returning GIs. Their wartime experience of lighter European models had been good and they tended to head for these showrooms when they got back home.

It was a very modern motorcycle in every regard ... bar one. For some inexplicable reason it retained a side-valve top end. It arrived as a 750 cc but was quickly bumped up to 883 cc (referred to as a 55 inch or 900 cc) to make it more competitive with the British 500 OHVs. However, its complicated build – in terms of both engine and chassis – meant it wasn't cheap enough to make the impact that it should have.

What the K should have been emerged in 1957 in the X-Series, which was known from the beginning as the Sportster. Outwardly a K-series with an OHV top end, it was arguably the world's second superbike (the first being the British Vincent, the only bike known to show it a clean pair of heels). The cast iron and unit construction combination made unlikely bedfellows, but it worked well.

Barring an increase to 61 inches (1000 cc) and switching from a left to a right-foot gearshift in the early Seventies (and finally replacing the 12 volt generator with an alternator in the early Eighties), it survived remarkably untouched. Until it was reworked to create the Evo Sportster in 1986, that is. It finally got a five speed gearbox in 1992, rubber-mounting in 2004, and fuel injection in 2007. The motor still provides the foundation for not only the 2009 Sportsters and the new XR1200 but also the Buell XB-models.

And if that sounds unlikely, it's no more surprising than to learn that the side-valve K-series, withdrawn from the road range in 1957, was still campaigning ten years later in its TT guise. As you can read elsewhere in this publication, it won twelve of the seventeen national championships before it was finally replaced by the XR-750.

K-Series
1952-53: 742 cc / 45.5 ci (nominally 750 cc / 45 ci) side valve
1954-56: 888 cc / 54.2 ci (nominally 900 cc / 55 ci) side valve

X-Series ('Ironhead')
1957-71: 883 cc / 53.9 ci (nominally 900 cc / 55 ci) OHV
1972-85: 1000 cc / 61ci OHV

X-Series ('Evo')
1986 to date: 883 cc / 53 ci OHV
1986-88: 1100 cc / 67 ci OHV
1988 to date: 1200 cc / 74 ci OHV
1991: 5-speed gearbox and belt drive on some models
2004: 'rubber-mount' frame

SHOVELHEAD
1966-86

F-Series

1966-1980: (1200 cc / 74 ci)
1978-1984: (1340 cc / 80 ci)
1971: FX Street range using XL forks
1979: FLHT 'rubber-mount' chassis/
5 speed gearbox
1983: FXR ' rubber-mount' chassis/
5-speed gearbox

If the Panhead had a hard act to follow, it was nothing compared to the challenge facing the Shovelhead. Starting off as an Electra Glide it was the first F-series to not have a kick-start as standard. Back then there wasn't the wealth of models that we know today; in fact, you got an Electra Glide with options or you bought a Sportster.

The Shovelhead's rocker cover again inspired its unofficial moniker, and this time it was held away from the top of the cylinder head, enough to provide a channel of cooling air between them, and it developed more power than the Panhead before it. For a generation of riders though it was synonymous more with the AMF years when many traditional production methods were dragged kicking and screaming into the latter part of the twentieth century, and while it symbolised a great many unpopular 'lasts' as well as evolutionary 'firsts', it established a solid foundation for Harley-Davidson's future.

Mechanically, it was the last of the 'generator' motors, with their DC dynamos situated at the front of the motor, hooked to the end of the crank by a series of gears, and which was replaced with an alternator on the drive-side. It was also the last F-series with a distributor. That was replaced by a set of points in a simple nose cone where the kidney-shaped timing chest used to live. And when it passed, it was the last of the classic Hemi motors.

The Shovelhead motor was in that frame when the foot shift/hand clutch became standard, and foot clutch/hand shift an option; when sand-cast cases gave way to die cast, and when industrial pragmatism was applied to the sourcing of parts, leading to Showa forks and Hitachi starter motors. It was also the time when production increased from 15,475 American-made heavyweights to over 50,000.

More importantly, it was the engine that saw the massive diversification of F-series models from an FL or an FLH to more than a dozen, based on seven distinct models, much of which is a result of the inspired decision to marry lightweight Sportster cycle parts to the Shovelhead motor and frame to create the FX Super Glide – and to which Harley-Davidson in 2009 owes its very existence.

It saw the introduction of the 5-speed gearbox, the rubber-mounted power train, belt primary and final drives, electronic ignition and the rise and rise of the factory custom. It also saw the return of an old friend in the 80-inch motor, which ran alongside the 74-inch FL ... but didn't become the GL because that would have made it a Gold Wing.

EVOLUTION
1984-2000

FROM 1984 TO 2000

EIGHTY CUBIC INCHES

V²

THE EVO

F-Series
1984-1999: (1340 cc / 74 ci)
1984: FXST range using 'Softail' frame
1991: FXD range using Dyna frame
1994: FLHR Road King family

With a production overlap at each end, the next stage of Harley-Davidson's evolution was the Evolution motor. This was shortened to the Evo motor for most, or the Blockhead for those who felt an urge to continue with the vernacular naming conventions.

Produced alongside the Shovel for the first two years of its life, the 80-inch Evo motor continued the process of regular top-end engine fixes. There wasn't much wrong with the alternator bottom end, but the Hemi motor had run its course as far as the technology of the time and EPA pressures were concerned. A flat-top piston with a bathtub-shaped combustion chamber replaced the dome within a dome, and words like 'squish' were used to describe the more efficient, cleaner-burning motor.

Without any hint of irony, while it was the motor that was born of pragmatism – the new die-cast aluminium barrels lacking the traditional, near-sculpted contours of the cast iron barrels of the Shovelhead and Evo – its power delivery, courtesy of the bore and stroke of the 80-inch Shovel, was pure Harley-Davidson. The 'Hear No Evo, See No Evo, Ride No Evo' T-shirts were massively outnumbered

by the factory-licensed clothing of a whole new generation of Harley riders, as well as many eager converts from the traditional market.

Almost everyone embraced the twenty-first century Harley-Davidson engine. It was a motor that ran cool, didn't leak, didn't rattle, had massive potential for tuning and even though it was strangled by EPA emissions regulations from the factory gate, was easily liberated by the application of a little knowledge.

With the Evo motor, Harley-Davidson hit the mainstream and it was a brave new independent Harley-Davidson that capitalised on their new dawn. While it might have been the Shovelhead the saw the introduction of a breadth of new models, the Evo saw those bikes find their owners.

A marketing as well as a mechanical masterpiece, the Evo was treated to Harley-Davidson's first attempts at fuel injection and saw many minor fixes through its lifetime. It was its partnership with the Softail frame that established it as most modern Harley riders' classic big twin motor – even if they loved it more for its appearance than its un-damped sensory feedback. The sheer number of clones produced across America bears testament to its continuing popularity.

TWIN CAM
1999-DATE

FROM 1999 TO PRESENT DAY

Harley could have been seen as riding high on the hog as the new millennium approached, but despite the sniping from their critics, they've actually always kept pace with technology. They've just used that technology to create the bikes they want to make. In 1999, we saw the first break with the fundamentals of the bottom end that they first unveiled in 1936.

There was only so much they could do in terms of the combustion chamber with the valve angles they had to work with, and those valve angles were dictated by the rocker arms, which were determined by the angle of the pushrods. They'd messed about as far as they could at the top of the pushrod, which left the bottom. There wasn't much room for manoeuvre at the bottom either, its position dictated by the single camshaft, so they split it into two. It was that or an overhead cam and that would have been very brave. They'd done it before with the Knucklehead's predecessor in the 1928/29 Two Cam, and the 1999 Twin Cam 88 was the result ... for two-thirds of the F-series range.

Abbreviated by the factory to be the TC88, the new motor became the Fathead to a dwindling bunch of people who didn't already have enough model names to wrap their tongues around. The engine was slotted into the Dyna and Touring ranges, isolated from the frame in the now-traditional rubber-mounts. But the higher-revving power characteristic of the bigger-bore 88-inch motor didn't lend itself to the solid-mounted and much more traditional Softail. The solution was the TC88B in 2000, with the B standing for balance shafts. Still bolted firmly into the frame, the balance shafts counteract the secondary vibration from the 45-degree v-twin, making it run substantially smoother than it otherwise would – right up to the sort of revs that a Softail has no right to investigate, at which point it gets a little tingly.

The Twin Cam 88 has a greater sense of sophistication compared to Harley's long-stroke heritage, which was well-received by the newer riders. There's nothing like stump-pulling torque to sum up the experience of a proper American engine – and in 2007 the Twin Cam got a stroker crank and a boost to 96-cubic inches, bringing with it a return to long stroke engine characteristics and the opportunity to

F-Series
1999-2006: Twin Cam 88: 1450 cc/88 ci – FXD/FLHR/FLHT only
2000-2007: Twin Cam 88B: 1450 cc/88 ci – balanced for FXST
2007 to date: Twin Cam 96 / 96B

fit a big bore kit to get a 103-inch capacity for those who want even more. But then the 96-inch Twin Cam came with a 5-speed gearbox and an evolved fuel injection system that is a massive improvement upon the strangled Evo in factory trim. It made the modification of an air box and exhaust more a personal search for aural gratification than the creation of a viable motorcycle from one strangled by regulation and legislation.

Where next for the Harley-Davidson Big Twin? If the rumours are true, we won't have long to wait to find out.

VR SERIES
2001-DATE

FROM 2001 to PRESENT DAY
VR-SERIES

VR-Series

2002-2007: 1130 cc Revolution DOHC
liquid-cooled
2008 to date: 1250 cc Revolution DOHC
liquid-cooled

For a company best known for its lazy cruisers, Harley has certainly got a lot of racing heritage. XR-750s are still successfully campaigning on the oval tracks and TT courses of America, and back in 1994 Harley-Davidson fancied their chances back on the Daytona bankings. They made a bid for Superbike success with an all-new engine; the VR1000.

A liquid-cooled, DOHC short-stroke 60-degree V-twin, it was developed with help from Porsche, but failed to make an impression on a massively competitive race series. Rumours continued right through until 2001 of a possible resurrection of the VR1000 though … right up until, that is, the sheets were pulled back on the most radical new Harley-Davidson ever seen. Called the VRSCA or V-Rod, it looked like a concept bike, but was indeed a production model. Hours of TV time were given to tell its story, making it perhaps the most easily identifiable brand new motorcycle of the decade.

The rough-hewn but functional VR1000 motor had been cosmetically tweaked to better suit the factory's image, but there was no disguising its heritage. A full unit construction motor – with the gearbox and crankshaft in a common case – its pistons slide in wet liners within barrels cast into the top of the horizontally split crankcases. It couldn't be further from traditional Harley-Davidson engineering practices without doubling the number of pistons and sticking them in a straight line. Rubber-mounted and counterbalanced for smoothness, with twin downdraft velocity stacks feeding its electronic fuel injection, it was immediately apparent that this would be a Harley-Davidson motor of the future. Just not the future of the mainstay model ranges though. It's far too busy mechanically, and has completely the wrong power characteristics to satisfy existing markets.

Tuned for sheer horsepower rather than torque, its tacho needle hurtles round its half-moon dial with indecent pace before burying itself into the redline at 9,000rpm before its rev limiter cuts in. This has created a new role for it … although, to turn that on its head, it's more likely the role provided the impetus for the production bike. While the Superbike programme has been brushed under the carpet, the V-Rod has enjoyed spectacular success in drag racing, where its length and explosive power serves it very well.

AH

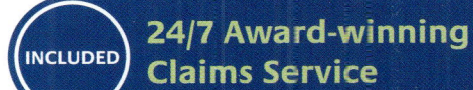

RACING THE BLACK, WHITE AND ORANGE

From the moment that the motorcycle was invented it was a foregone conclusion that the second man with a bike would race against the first man with a bike. And of course, they did. Metaphorically speaking, and often literally too, in the United States of America one of the first bikes was Indian and one of the second was Harley-Davidson. And guys have been racing Harleys in as many different ways as you can imagine. As many ways as there are different styles of bikes – and more. To the best of my knowledge, no one races full-dress Ultra Glides, but apart from that ...

Motordrome or board track racing, as it became known, was one of the original forms of organised motorcycle competition and grew from the huge interest in push bike racing in the late 1800s. These races took place on banked wooden tracks called Velodromes where upwards of 10,000 spectators (no TV or computer games around in those days) came along to watch men in tights, with large moustaches and bulging calf muscles, race around in circles on pedal cycles.

To increase the speed of the bicycles by reducing the wind resistance, they used bigger bicycles fitted with new fangled internal ▶

combustion engines. These weren't to race, but to ride in front of the pedal bikes to 'break the wind' (as it were). The riders sat bolt upright, often with a vertical wooden board behind them called a coupe vent, or wind break.

Popularised in Europe, especially in France where the Velodrome is claimed to have originated, it was only a matter of time before someone realised that it would be a lot more exciting to watch the motorised pacer bikes race around the track than the pedal bikes.

As I say, racing had been around since motorcycles were invented, mostly as long and gruelling events on public roads, but this was a chance to make money out of it. Board track racing was somewhat short-lived in Europe, but in America it was phenomenally successful. Many of the early riders, like the Indian racer Ralf Di Palma, were former pushbike racers, and most early top-speed records were made on board tracks by the likes of the famous Super-X rider, Joe Petrali (whose name you'll find elsewhere in this bookazine).

One of the most reliable pace bikes on the US board tracks was made by Oscar Hedstrom and Charles Henshaw. At a race in Springfield, Massachusetts around the turn of the century, the owner of the Velodrome, George Hendee, approached Hedstrom and Henshaw with the notion of racing the pace bikes against each other. The partnership that was formed out of that meeting, however, was to last a lot longer than board-track racing. This is because it was the affiliation of Hendee and Hedstrom, who later founded the Indian Motorcycle Company in Springfield in 1905.

It was Hendee's track manager, Jack Prince, who built the first of the tracks suitable for high-speed motorcycle racing. That was in 1908. These board tracks, as the name suggests, were made out of two-by-four inch wooden planks. They were a quarter to one third of a mile in length, and had steeply banked angles on the corners of up to 62 degrees (by comparison the banking at the Daytona Speedway is 31 degrees), where the bikes could reach speeds in excess of 90mph.

The exciting spectacle of board-track racing was born, and Prince went on to spend seventeen years building tracks all over the USA. 'Exciting spectacle' however usually meant thrills and spills, and a fatal accident in 1912 that killed two riders and six spectators led to many of these short, steeply banked board tracks being closed. No-one really minded too much if it was the riders who were getting killed, after all, that was what they were getting paid for and they knew the risks involved. When the paying punters were getting slaughtered by runaway motorcycles though, well, that was bad for business. To make the racing safer (and so that it would be more difficult for the spectators to get injured), longer and less steeply banked board tracks were built. These were up to two miles long, though the majority were one mile in length.

Sadly, none of the old board tracks exist today, but period film and photos show that these tracks were huge – easily the width of a dual carriageway (what our American cousins would call a four-lane highway). Speeds of 110mph were possible; in fact the absolute lap record on a board track was held by Jim Davis on a Harley-Davidson at 110.67mph, and was never beaten. Davis was one of the most successful American motorcycle racers of all time, and won championships from all three organisations that sanctioned the sport at that time in America; The Federation of American Motorcyclists, Motorcycle and Allied Trades Association and – the only one that has stood the test of time – the American Motorcyclist Association.

It was on the board tracks that the basics of slipstreaming was

Top: Harley introduced their first V-twin in 1909 and it soon made its way on to the race track.
Middle: The single cylinder engine survived though, as on this 1928 Peashooter board racer.
Bottom: And these historic racers are still turning up in barns; fancy a restoration project?

Top: Board racer (with no brakes!) had a primitive fairing and a pad on the tank for the rider to lie on.
Middle and Bottom: Beautifully restored 1928 factory racer with the tall, 21 cubic inch single cylinder motor

learned and because the tracks were made from wood it was possible to race in all weathers: In fact, damp conditions were preferred by the riders as it swelled the wood, making the boards tighter and the track faster. In the parts of America where it didn't rain very often, the local fire brigade was often called in to wet down the boards a few hours before the race. Racing on a wooden track had disadvantages though – such as riders (and occasionally spectators) being hit by splinters as big as pencils. Accidents are often cited as being the reason that board track racing fell from grace, but every fad has its peak. Also, due to the sheer size of the tracks, the maintenance costs were high and by the end of the 1920s board-track racing had all but disappeared in the USA.

The stock market crash of 1929 affected almost every facet of life in USA, and by 1933, of the three hundred American motorcycle manufacturers that had produced machines at some time or another

The battles between Harleys and Indians on the racetrack during the 1930s became legendary

since the turn of the century, only two remained standing.

Times were hard, and to sell their wares the last two indigenous manufacturers, Harley-Davidson and Indian, faced up to each other on the racetrack. Just as today among almost all motorcycle manufacturers (except, ironically, Harley-Davidson and the revitalised Indian company), success in sport spells sales from the showroom floor. The battles between Harleys and Indians on the racetrack during the 1930s became legendary. But, fierce as the competition was, motorcycle racing in America was also in decline due to the rules and regulations of the period, which made it difficult and expensive for the would-be part-time and amateur racer to take part. American Motorcycle Association (AMA) racing at the time was little more than a battle between the two factories, and as such the rules were more or less dictated by the hierarchy of Harley-Davidson and Indian. Their strategy was to keep any imported machines at a disadvantage, with regulations that favoured the two American manufacturers. Both factories hired professional racers, and both factories produced very specialised machines. Many of these bore little resemblance to their road-going products, which was a double-edged formula that was both expensive and was increasingly alienating to the paying public.

While race teams like the Harley-Davidson Wrecking Crew battled it out with Indian and Excelsior on the dirt tracks, with expensive and exclusive factory-produced large capacity V-twins such as the famous eight-valve race bikes, a less expensive form of motorcycle competition started to become popular in both Great Britain and the USA. This had originated in New Zealand using (mostly) small capacity single-cylinder machines, and the sport came to be known as speedway. Although the declining AMA 21 cubic inch class had ▶

originally been rejuvenated by both Excelsior and Indian, who both had 350 cc roadsters to base their proposed 21ci race bikes on, it was the OHV version of Harley-Davidson's quickly-produced 1926 model AA 350 cc single that dominated the class. (The side-valve version was the Model A, while the B and AB models of the same bikes respectively featured electric lights).

Known as the Peashooter, the modified model A featured a shortened wheelbase version of the roadster frame, with strutted telescopic forks based on an earlier design by Fred Merkel on his Flying Merkel motorcycles. The Peashooter used a simple countershaft to transfer the primary drive to the rear wheel instead of a conventional gearbox. The bikes were also equipped with narrow spoked wheels – and were bereft of brakes. There was also an absence of all road-going equipment. With its good handling and high power-to-weight ratio, the Peashooter had eclipsed all other forms of competition on the short track and speedway circuits by 1928 ... not only in the USA and Great Britain, but also in New Zealand and Australia where the sport had originated.

Featuring exposed valve gear, the top-end of the 350 cc OHV single-cylinder engine needed constant attention to keep it in tune, but on a race bike this was no great detriment. The roadster-based engine could only be tuned so far however, and by 1930 the Peashooter's dominance was ending. It was soon being pushed down the field by purpose-built JAP and Rudge-engined bikes. Racing always breeds hybrids of course, and one of the most successful speedway bikes of the 1930s was the JAP-engined Comerford-Wallis. This featured a modified Harley Peashooter frame, fitted with a version of the same primitive Flying Merkel derived Harley-Davidson telescopic front forks, with their full one inch of spring-loaded travel. A few Comerford-Wallis JAP-engined bikes were exported to the USA, where no doubt American racers had also been slotting the mechanical products of the JA Prestwich Manufacturing Company into their Peashooters.

Not be outdone by the Limey interlopers, Harley-Davidson set about producing a new 500 cc speedway bike with a heat-treated chrome-molybdenum frame, a one-piece cast aluminium fuel/oil tank and an OHV engine. This motor was so close to the JAP in outside dimensions that it could be swapped over without modification. The interior workings of the new 500 cc Harley OHV engine were a different matter though, and only about a dozen prototype machines were produced before the project was shelved. JAP-engined Peashooters continued to be popular on both sides of the Atlantic, and while the sport of speedway became hugely popular in Europe right into the 1960s, by the end of the 1930s it had been overshadowed in the USA by dirt-track racing. It was this branch of two-wheeled competition that saw the re-emergence of the large capacity V-twin engine as a dominant tour de force.

Motorcycle racing in 1930s America followed three different paths: flat track, speedway and hill climbs. Flat track (or dirt track) was much the same as it is today, with specialised bikes racing around a prepared mile or half-mile oval track that could trace its origin back to the days of horse and buggy racing at the local fairground. Held on smaller, tighter ovals than dirt track, speedway was very similar to the European version of the sport. Hill climbing was exactly what it sounds like – racing motorcycles up a big hill. There were other forms of motorcycle competition such as TT racing – which was more akin to modern motocross than the TT name suggests – and road racing.

The latter took place on public roads ('roads' that were tarmac, dirt, grass or sand – and sometimes a mixture of all four). There were a few survivors of the old board racing tracks, but those were more of a fairground attraction than real competitive racing.

Just as Americans are sometimes wont to over-complicate any form of sport (look at how they've turned a simple kid's playground game like rounders into the baffling sport of baseball, or the schoolboy game of rugby into the incomprehensible statistical nightmare that is American football), so it was with motorcycle racing. There were Byzantine rules and regulations governing which capacity machine and which engine layout could take part in which of the many

Motorcycle racing in 1930s America followed three different paths; flat track, speedway and hill climbs

different forms of competition. Add to this the fact that the events were divided into two different rider classes, Class A for top echelon and professional riders and Class B for aspiring Class A riders and everybody else, and you can see why it was so difficult for a novice to take part. The answer was a new classification to cater for anyone and everyone who wanted to have a go on a cheap and easily available machine ... and the obvious name for the new category was Class C.

Class C is the original version of what we would call production racing today. Apart from a few modifications in the interest of safety, the bike has to be raced in the same spec as the manufacturer supplied it to the customer. Yeah right; if you've ever been involved in racing you'll know that this is about as likely as Pamela Anderson getting as Oscar for acting. The new Class C rules dictated that events could be contested by stock production motorcycles with

an engine displacement of 45 cubic inches (750 cc) if they were side valve, and 30.50 cubic inches (500 cc) if they were of overhead valve configuration. No surprise there then. Both Harley-Davidson and Indian were producing – and already racing – machines that fitted right into that niche. The rules of Class C also required the manufacturer to produce at least twenty five machines before it was eligible for the class, and the model had to be in the manufacturer's catalogue and on offer to the public in a fully roadworthy format. In addition, the manufacturer had to provide the AMA with a fully detailed list of model specification (so that they could spot the cheaters), and the rider had to own the machine (and have the paperwork to prove it), and ride the bike to and away from the event. Actually, this last rule didn't last too long.

Class C racing was born in 1933, and to take part both Harley-Davidson and Indian converted their existing 75 occ side-valve V-twins to be eligible to race in the new series. Indian produced a hot version of their famous 750 cc 101 Scout, and Harley devotees had a choice of the ordinary 45 cubic inch W, the high compression WL or the WLD sports solo. The competition in this new class between production machines from Harley-Davidson and Indian was as fierce as it had been in previous year with the earlier, pukka factory race bikes. In 1937, Harley moved the battle with Indian up a gear and introduced the WLDR, a true blue scalp-hunter with a full-on roller

bearing engine and special aluminium cylinder heads. Two years later, the model was re-designated as the WLDD, and in 1940 its moniker was changed again to WLD. The WLDR title was given to a model that, although it had a factory-tuned race engine also, rather confusingly, had full road-going equipment such as lights and brakes.

Thankfully the WL model confusion ended a year later when Harley introduced the WR and its derivatives. The WR was, despite what it said on the spec list, a fully fledged race bike – without lights, a horn or even brakes. Despite its archaic side-valve engine it continued the fight against the Indians, and the goddam foreign imports, right into the 1950s. After the end of WW2 Harley-Davidson wasted no time in getting the WR back into production, and although only a hundred examples of the race-tuned 45 ci side-valve V-twins were produced by the Milwaukee factory from pre-war parts that year, the Harley race department was back in business.

The KR750 was the race version of the new K-model roadster, and was launched by Harley-Davidson in 1952. The K-model featured all that was current in contemporary motorcycle design – swinging-arm rear suspension, hydraulically damped telescopic forks and a unit construction engine featuring alloy cylinder heads. Amazingly for what was in reality an all-new motorcycle though, Harley-Davidson had decided to make the engine a side-valve. Even in 1952 apart from bikes that time forgot – like the BSA M20 – side-valve motorcycles ▶

There were a few survivors of the old board racing tracks, but those were more of a fairground attraction than real competitive racing

were as dead as George III. However, despite being hampered with a side-valve engine, the KR was a capable racer (partly thanks to the OHV opposition being restricted to 500 cc). It raced competitively right into the latter half of the 1960s. Even when the capacity ruling was changed, the KR still managed to hold its own occasionally against the 650 and 750 cc overhead valve Triumph, BSA and Norton twins.

In spite of this, Harley and the AMA had an ace up their collective sleeves. It was one which would give the old Flatheads a last gasp, and that was a bigger cube KR. On the racetrack the KR750 was joined by the KHR – an 883 cc long-stroke development of the KR. The stroke of the engine was increased from 3.8125 inches to 4.5625 inches by changing the flywheels, just as Harley had done to increase the swept volume of the KH900 roadsters. And as with the KRs, the KHR came with a rigid rear-end for dirt track racing, while the KHRTT had a swinging-arm with shock absorbers for TT and road racing. The aforementioned 'last gasp' was that although this larger engine was only legal when raced in AMA open-class events (which usually consisted of bikes with 74 and 80 ci engines), as soon as

Harley-Davidson announced the new larger 883 cc engine the AMA upped the parameters from open to a top limit of 900 cc. This was approximately the same cubic capacity as Harley's new KHR. No surprises there then.

By the end of the 1960s the writing was on the wall for Harley's long suffering side-valves – at last – and the KR's swansong came in 1969 during the Daytona 200. Up against a swarm of Japanese factory two-strokes the late, great Cal Rayborn's KR750TT was the only four-stroke in the top-ten qualifiers for the 200 – and seven out of the ten of the Japanese bikes were Yamaha two-stroke twins. In the race itself, the superfast strokers either crashed or melted their engines, and Cal cruised home to win the Daytona 200 on a bike that was as outdated

500 cc against the side-valve Harley 750s, and OHC machines like the 500 cc Manx Norton were just banned after wiping the floor with everything. With their cubic capacity advantage now well out of the window, Harley looked to their 'new' 900cc OHV Sportster to provide a contender.

Nothing is ever really new where Harley-Davidson is concerned, and the 1957 XL Sportster was little more than an OHV version of the earlier KH side-valve. Mind you, that in itself was little more than a unit construction version of the side-valve 45 introduced in the 1930s with a 4-speed gearbox tacked on the back of a common crankcase. In order to get the 900 cc (actually 883 cc) Sportster engine down to the

By the end of the 1960s the writing was on the wall for Harley's long suffering side-valves

required 750 cc capacity limit, all that the H-D race department had to do was relocate the crankpin closer to the centre of the flywheels. This reduced the stroke from 3.812 inch to 3.219, while retaining the stock bore of 3.00 inch. This naturally meant shortening the cylinders and using the same connecting rods, high-lift cams and magneto as the earlier XLR full race version of the 1957 Sportster.

Harley-Davidson frames of the period were (and still are) big old heavy boat anchors, with the design of the frame tailored to accommodate aspects such as the convenient location of the saddlebags rather than efficient operation of the suspension. The only frame that Harley-Davidson had in production that had the rear shock absorbers in a position that actually worked was the Lowboy KRTT road race frame. No need for saddlebags, y'see? It was a relatively lightweight tubular steel frame, that also had the advantage of Ceriani forks (courtesy of H-D's Aermacchi Italian connection), and the iconic fibreglass fuel tank and seat unit that came by way of Harley's AMF parent company's involvement in manufacturing plastic-bodied golf buggies.

The basic 1969 XR-750 came without brakes, but with Girling rear shockers straight-through pipes, a roadster type 'ham can' air filter cover and a hole in the gearbox sprocket cover for a kick start lever. There was also a full complement of optional extras such as brakes, bigger fuel tanks and a full race fairing. The engine oil lived in a spring-mounted aluminium tank under the seat, and without fuel and oil it weighed in at a claimed 317lbs. The bike was launched in time for the start of the 1970 racing season, and the ever-partisan American motorcycle press raved about it. Harley-Davidson themselves called it the 'New 750 cc XR – Bad news for all other dirt track machines'.

The problem was that the only bad news was for anyone who'd bought an XR with hopes of winning races with it. The Harley-Davidson factory team were massacred at Daytona in 1970. All four works XR-750s melted their engines trying to run with the new crop ▶

as a stone axe.

Some bikes are born great, some bikes achieve greatness, and some bikes have greatness thrust upon them. In the case of the Harley-Davidson XR-750, all three are true ... well mostly true. It was the all-alloy version of the XR that can truly be accredited with all of the above, while the iron XR-750 was the bike that set the ball rolling. The iron XR-750 was born out of Harley-Davidson's need to come up with a three-quarter litre engine to comply with the new AMA rules. These allowed 750 cc bikes of any engine configuration to compete against each other in AMA racing. Prior to this rule change – in 1968 – the dice were loaded against any foreign opposition. They were either banning entirely or restricted in engine capacity. Any bike that came close to beating Harley-Davidson's esoteric and surprisingly fast side-valve 750 cc V-twins was simply ruled out of competition.

By the end of the Seventies though, the old, side-valve Harleys had no place in a modern world that was about to be blitzed by four-cylinder OHC Hondas, three-cylinder Triumphs and BSAs, and a horde of screaming two-stroke banshees from Yamaha and Kawasaki. OHV engines like the Triumph and BSA twins had been limited to

If you want some fun of a weekend, buy yourself a classic Harley and go racing. On the other hand (top right) if you want to scare yourself go for an XR 750, really well set up like this one (but remove handcuff from rear swinging arm before moving off!).

In 2006, one of the most desirable American race bikes
was offered for auction at Daytona Bike Week. J Wood &
Co. of Crystal River, Florida had Cal Rayborn's last XRTT up
for sale. Harley-Davidson had given the bike to Dick O'Brien, the
long-time manager of the factory team. It had been inherited by his
daughter, and she was offering it for sale, along with all its associated
documentation.

During his career Cal rode eighteen Harleys, of which six were
XRTTs. As I say, this was his last, and he raced it for the last time at
Ontario Speedway in 1973. Nothing had changed on the machine
since that day. There was even a mechanic's oily rag stuck into a
corner of the frame, and the fairing had been scorched by the exhaust
and not been repaired.

This was a real rarity, not just for its amazing history and
provenance, but because manufacturers' racers rarely come on to
the open market. They are often broken up by the factories' race
departments, as most XRTTs were. There was also the poignancy of
Cal's all-too-early death; he died on December 29 1973 at Pukekohe in
New Zealand, in what was a glorified Clubman event.

In the auction the bidding at Daytona was fierce, as you would
expect, and it was a mark of the affection and respect in which the
Rayborn name is still held that bike was sold for $160,000.

of 750 cc roadster-based multi-cylinder bikes from Europe and Japan. Although the iron XR-750 won its dirt track debut later the same year and it was constantly developed and improved, it would always prove troublesome. Its unreliability was due to the fact that it was a roadster-based engine with a top-end made out of the same heavy and heat-retaining material as an Aga oven.

The iron XR-750 was in production for two years, although it's very doubtful that any more were made apart from the two hundred examples initially manufactured to comply with the new AMA rules. For homologation that number of motorcycles had to be produced and inspected before the bike could be raced. There are many photographs of the iron XR-750 lined up in the factory's warehouse, although it's rumoured that many were lashed together just to make up the numbers. Very few of those XR-750s were sold – they didn't win races and nobody buys losers – and it's known that at least half of the two hundred were scrapped by H-D in the mid-Seventies.

If ever a motorcycle was built for a single purpose it was the all-alloy engine 1970 Harley-Davidson XR-750, and that purpose was flat-track racing. It was fast, furious, and as American as apple pie. Although Harley-Davidson did persist with road-race versions of the alloy XR-750 throughout the early 1970s, the writing was on the wall for the pavement Milwaukee pushrod twin and even the late great Calvin Rayborn had to eventually swap his Harley for a Suzuki. He simply tired of trailing the field. It was an unfortunate move because it cost him his life in 1972, when the Suzuki seized at high speed.

The XR-750 was built to keep the black, white and orange of The Motor Company in the winner's circle

The XR-750 engine is a crude and archaic device whose suitability to it specific application belies belief. The design of the engine is pure Harley; an inline air-cooled 45-degree V-twin with a pair of flywheels running in ball bearing mains. These were joined by a single crankpin holding a pair of blade-connecting rods in place with a caged roller bearing. The valve train layout follows a similar form and originates from Harley's early unit construction side-valve twin, although with two valves per cylinder, operated by long pushrods the valve train still consists of four single lobe camshafts in the lower-end gear case. These camshafts were now actuating four pushrods, transferring their action to the valves via four rocker arms mounted on two shafts in a separate bolt-on rocker boxes. Likewise, the transmission consists of a dry clutch in a wet primary case, driven by a triplex chain, and within a cavity behind the flywheel-housing, a cassette cluster of four forward gears. In other words, a 1970s adaptation of a 1950s design that remains virtually unchanged today.

The alloy XR-750 was built for one purpose only, and that was to keep the black, white and orange of The Motor Company in the winner's circle at the AMA dirt-track championship. Although

Yamaha and Honda did eventually develop race and Championship winning machines (albeit at huge financial cost), it was the Harley-Davidson XR-750 that filled the grid at the vast majority of AMA dirt track races – from its introduction right up to the present day. The Harley-Davidson XR-750 has won everything that there is to be won in AMA dirt-track racing. It is claimed to hold the title of the World's Most Successful Racing Engine. Beautiful from any angle and packing a twin-cylinder punch, the XR-750 is the epitome of the competition motorcycle. Lean, mean and loud, it came in one colour only – International Harvester orange – and it was, and still is, the best-looking motorcycle that Harley-Davidson has ever made.

In 1970, lying flat on his back with no forward vision, Calvin Rayborn took a Harley-Davidson-powered streamliner to a new world record of 266.785 mph, with an average two-way speed of 265.492 mph at the Bonneville Salt Flats. He later said that 1970 had been a bad year and he only did it for the money. The event was recorded on film and is featured in the well-known motorcycle documentary On Any Sunday, which tells how Calvin arrived at Bonneville and couldn't fit into the 25 inch-high streamliner without cutting the lower edge of his helmet away. The film really is an amazing testament to Rayborn's courage. The unwieldy streamliner crashed many times, once at 200 mph and rolled over thirty-five times before sliding to a standstill. The crew simply turned it around and Calvin was ready to try again.

Despite years of trying to regain its former success on the racetrack with brave attempts like Lucifer's Hammer, which actually did win races and ended the European domination of the BoTT (Battle of the

Jay Springsteen remains one America's greatest racers, and – needless to say – a Harley-Davidson hero

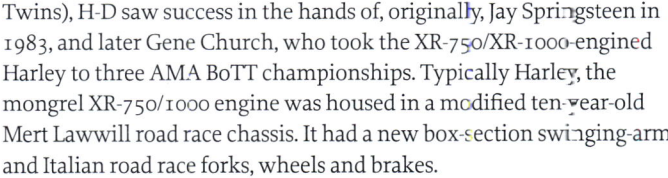

Twins), H-D saw success in the hands of, originally, Jay Springsteen in 1983, and later Gene Church, who took the XR-750/XR-1000-engined Harley to three AMA BoTT championships. Typically Harley, the mongrel XR-750/1000 engine was housed in a modified ten-year-old Mert Lawwill road race chassis. It had a new box-section swinging-arm and Italian road race forks, wheels and brakes.

This Italian connection was nothing new, however, as Harley-Davidson had bought an interest in the Italian Aermacchi company in the early 1960s in order to provide a lightweight single-cylinder bike into the Harley range. One of the immediate advantages was the legitimate use of the Italian company's forks and brakes on Harley's KR750 road racers. Called the Sprint in the USA, the re-badged 250/350 Aermacchi singles were popular on the race track. Well, until the advent of the Japanese two-strokes that is, though the bike remained competitive in European Grand Prix racing for much longer.

The early 1990s also saw a few seasons of Sportster racing in both the USA and Europe. That proved to be popular for a couple of years – especially as it was obvious that a Harley was going to win every time. But while it was popular with Harley dealers and some race fans, it was a bit like going to the racetrack in a Ferrari to watch the buses race.

Harley's last gasp at V-twin domination of AMA Superbike racing was the VR1000 that thundered around the racetrack in the latter half of the 1990s. Too heavy, too slow and too late – and despite a talented number of factory riders such as Chris Carr, Thomas Wilson, Doug Chandler, Scott Russell and Pascal Picotte – the VR1000 never

In common with Harley-Davidson, Coca-Cola and basketball, drag racing is a true blue American product

won a race and managed to finish very few. Ironically, after years of competing with a four-stroke V-twin against the Japanese factories who fielded motorcycles with every conceivable engine configuration, the World Superbike road race championship has been dominated by four-stroke V-twins for the past few years ... although none of them are Harley-Davidsons.

While it's true that the contemporary archetypal image of the Harley-Davidson motorcycle is more in the vein of cruising and snoozing rather than balls-out thundering performance, you don't have to look to far in order to find Harleys that are fast enough to make your eyes bleed. We are, of course, talking about drag racing – a sport that to the outsider seems to consist of spending the largest amount of money possible on a motorcycle ... in order to ride it for the shortest possible time.

In common with Harley-Davidson, Coca-Cola and basketball, drag racing is a true blue American product, and in reality it is the simplest and probably the earliest form of motorcycle competition. All you need is a straight piece of road and somebody to race against. Although now somewhat complicated with different types of ▸

431
HARLEY-DAVIDSON OF LAKELAND
SHOEI
CYCLE

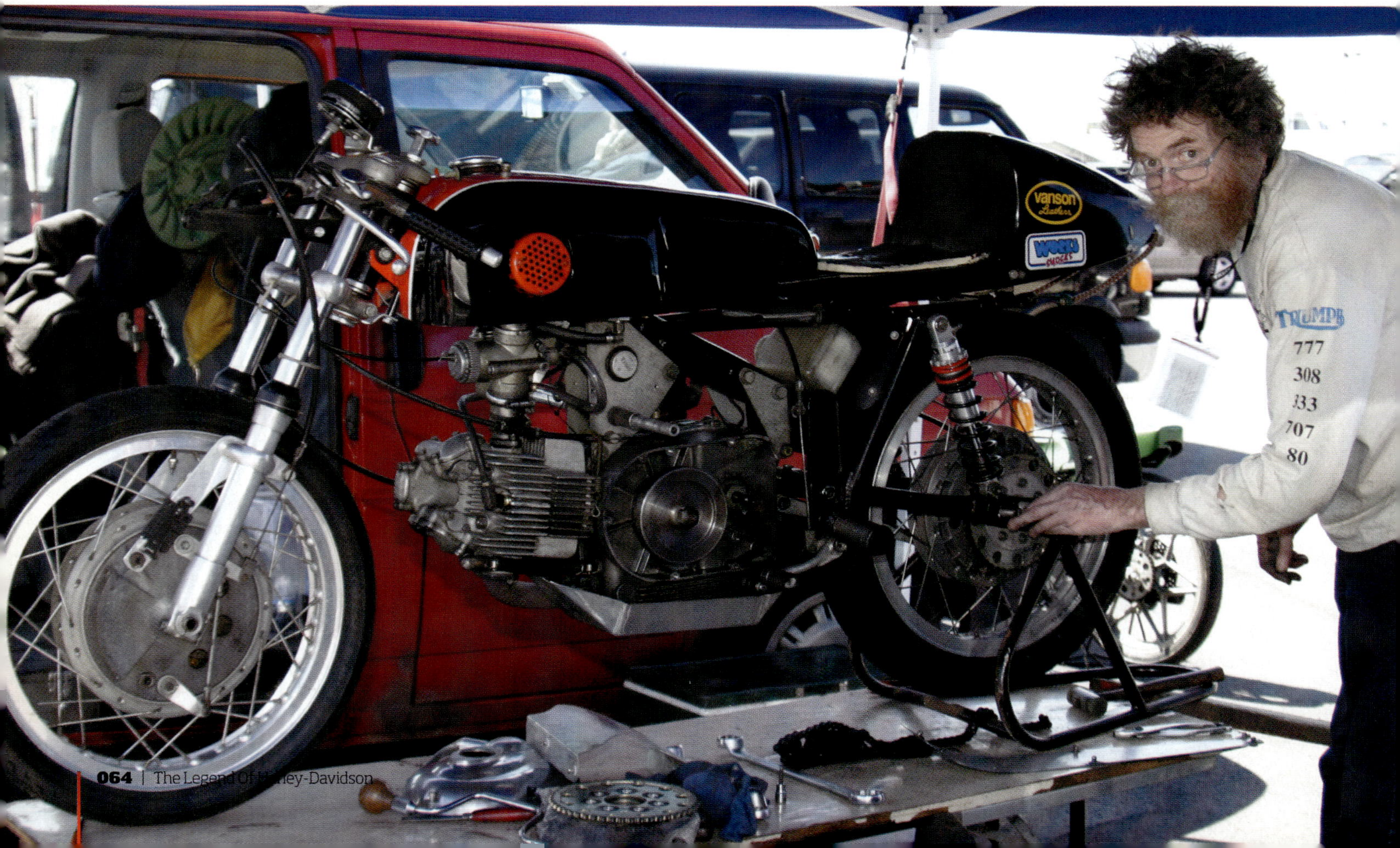
vanson
TRIUMPH
777
308
707
80

Left: Come the Seventies, come the Italian connection, and the Aermacchi-derived lightweights brought a whole new dimension to Harley-Davidson racing.
This page: In drag racing there's a class for every Harley enthusiast who wants to go racing, from street legal to pro stock

The only bad news was for anyone who'd bought an XR with hopes of winning races with it

handicap and bracket racing, the main objective in a drag race is to get to the other end of the quarter mile stretch of tarmac, from a standing start, before the other guy. Easy to understand and fun to watch – as all of the action takes place within the first hundred feet of the start line - it's in this relatively straightforward straight-line sport that a Harley-Davidson can still excel. The esoteric V-twin engine configuration is actually an asset rather than a hindrance.

America is obviously the home of Harley-Davidson drag racing, and although many Harleys compete successfully against imported motorcycles in many drag racing classes, it's in the one-make competitions organised by the likes of the All Harley Drag Racing Association (AHDRA) that all manner of Milwaukee metal take to the track to compete against each other. This format has been around, albeit under a few different names, for the past twenty five years. Similar organisations in Australia and in Europe were also formed to promote both Harley and twin-cylinder drag racing. Very

popular in Holland, Germany and Scandinavia, the All Harley Drags is a German-based series that takes place throughout Europe, while the Scandinavian Super Twins Series is, predictably, dominated by Scandinavian riders riding both Harley-based bikes and many other twin-cylinder designs of their own manufacture.

From a spectator's viewpoint it's the Top Fuel bikes that are the main attraction at any all-Harley event. These are ground-shaking, nitro-burning twin cylinder monsters that tear up the track at over 200mph, with mid-six-second quarter-mile times. Okay, so maybe while all of these nitro-snorting behemoths are called Harley-Davidsons, it's most likely the only part on the whole motorcycle that originally hails from the Milwaukee factory is the name on the petrol tank. To the delighted, partisan crowd who come and witness the spectacle though, a Harley is a Harley is a Harley regardless. But, and especially so in the United States, it's the lower echelons in the various all-Harley drag racing series that have the most competitors. In fact there's a ▶

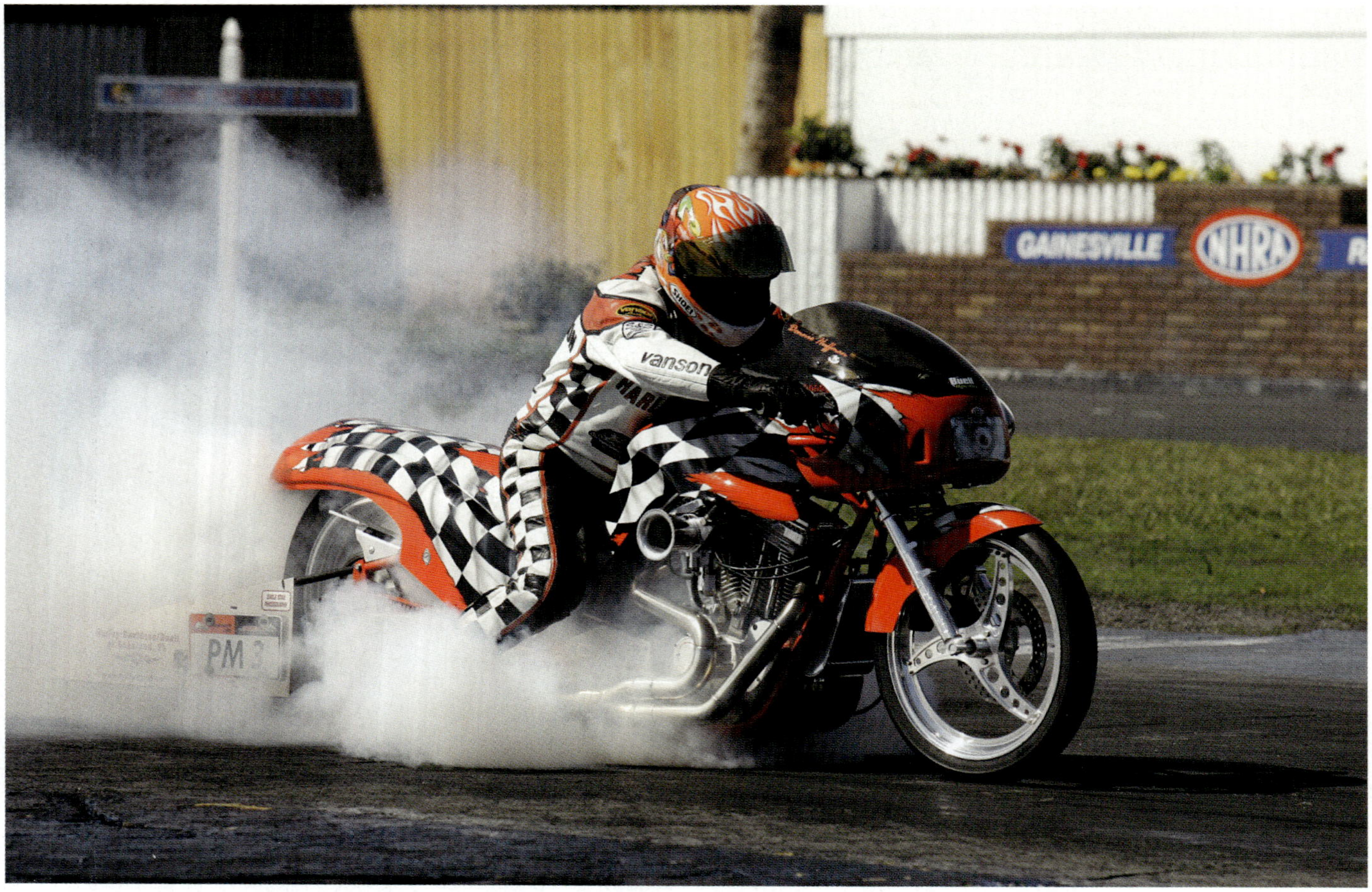
GAINESVILLE
NHRA
vanson
PM 3

ESVILLE RACEWAY

VANCE HINES

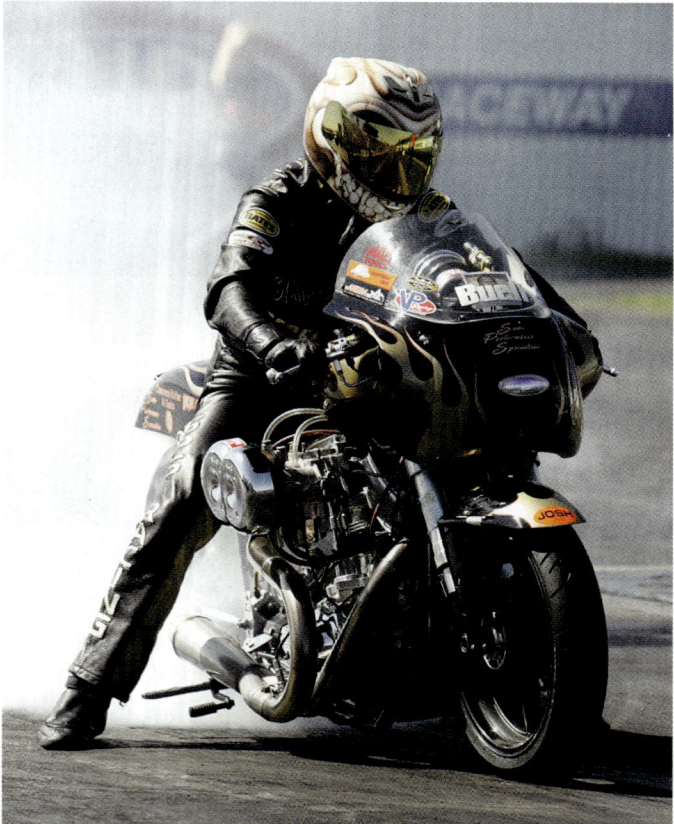

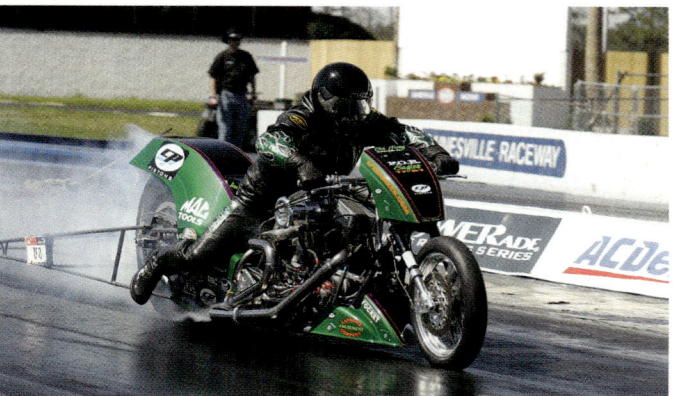

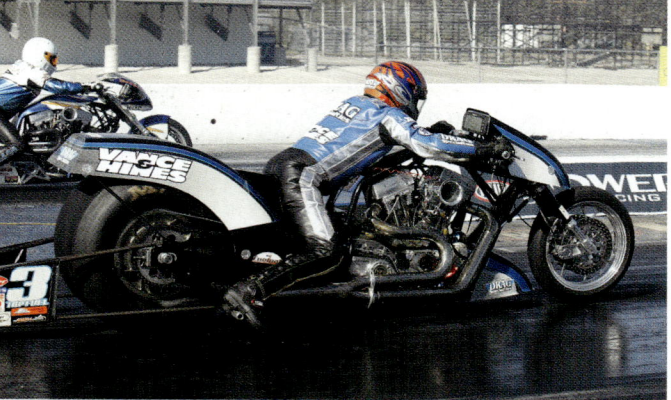

class for anyone who wants to go racing; from street legal to street modified to pro stock (with even individual classes for Sportsters, Dressers, Buells and V-Rods). That's long before you get to the heady nitro-methanol and mega-expensive world of Top Fuel racing.

Gainesville Raceway in northern Florida is home to the AHDRA extravaganza during Bike Week. It's a quarter-mile strip of wall-to-wall V-twin thunder. The Harley-Davidson drag racing circus comes to town for two days during Bike Week; travelling from all over the United States to partake in the red-line feeding frenzy. I'm talking Street, Super Street, Pro-Stock and many other diverse classes like old timers and Screamin' Eagle Destroyers. The cherry on the top of the pie is the nasty and noisy ultimate speed fix of Top-Fuel. Using more fuel to cover one-quarter mile than an F16 blasting off an aircraft carrier deck, a pair of nitro-burning Top-Fuel Harley-Davidsons take off down the strip as one. In a fight to the finish, the ground shakes, your ears bleed, and a smile a mile wide covers your face. Believe me, friends, you haven't experienced motorcycle drag racing until you've been blitzed by a pair of Top-Fuel Harleys ridden in anger. And you know what? Nowadays, when it comes to racing, it's definitely what Harley does best. **BC**

You haven't experienced motorcycle drag racing until you've been blitzed by a pair of Top-Fuel Harleys ridden in anger

Words & Photos: Bob Clarke
Thanks to Dale Walksler at The Wheels Through Time American Transport Museum, Maggie Valley, NC 28751, USA.
Website: www.wheelsthroughtime.com

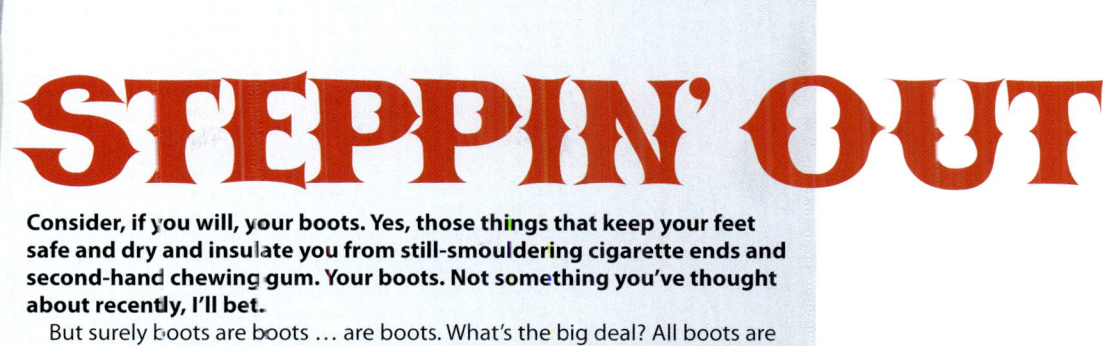

STEPPIN' OUT

Consider, if you will, your boots. Yes, those things that keep your feet safe and dry and insulate you from still-smouldering cigarette ends and second-hand chewing gum. Your boots. Not something you've thought about recently, I'll bet.

But surely boots are boots … are boots. What's the big deal? All boots are much the same. Well, you could say that all motorcycles are the same, but you don't think that, or else you wouldn't be reading this magazine. There are motorcycles, and then there are Harley-Davidsons. Similarly, there are boots, and then there are Radical boots.

Radical are different. For a start they're better made than any other boot on the market, and they look better too; stylish, distinctive and individual. They're the custom Harleys of the boot world.

Run your fingers over a Radical boot some time (but perhaps not when someone is wearing them, unless you're invited to do so …) and you might well be surprised to find that the designs are actually three-dimensional. The textures and images are, to use the sculptural term, in relief. I told you we're talking quality, now didn't I?

The designs you see on a Radical boot aren't merely silk screen printed on to the leather either, or – worse still – ironed on. The Radical images are impressed into the leather, so you can be sure that they are there for keeps. They won't fade or rub off. They won't crack or peal. As long as the leather lasts, the design will last too. And that's going to be really long time. Best make sure that your children grow up to have the same foot size as yourself; these boots might just be the modern equivalent of your grandfather's half-hunter gold watch …

The high level of quality extends to the construction of the boots too. These boots are well made - and made to last - by highly experienced Mexican craftsmen who fashion every boot individually. The soles are stitched to the uppers, not just glued, so when the soles wear they can be replaced again and again. And Radical know that these boots have to work hard, which is why the soles are oil and grease resistant, and are non-slip too. I suspect you won't be surprised to learn that they're all water-proof too.

Every single Radical boot is made out of the very highest quality leather. Second rate leather isn't an option! Fine calf leather is used to line the uppers of the boots as well.

There are four distinct – and distinctly different – ranges of Radical boots; Biker boots (of course), the Phoenix range, the Western boots and the Exotic Skin range. This last group of eleven styles include crocodile skin, ostrich and lizard – so that word exotic is no exaggeration.

Radical boots are available for men and women, in a broad range of sizes. The company recommend that you take four separate measurements of your feet to ensure a really good fit, and you'll find those, along with full details and photos of the whole range at radicalbootco.co.uk. Be warned though, you'll come off the site wanting at least a couple of pairs … or three. Or four. Or maybe a whole wardrobe full.

For more information on Radical Boots go to www.radicalbootco.co.uk or call 01423 504444

Words: Steven Myatt
Photos: Horst Rösler
Bruce Springsteen photo: Reuters

THE BIG 105

They'd come from all over the USA – and indeed from even further away. The factory had organised 'homecoming' rides from 105 American cities, all funnelled along twenty five major routes and timed to arrive at Milwaukee on the same day. Those furthest away left home on August 17 and they were all at Milwaukee exactly ten days later. The number of departure points was appropriate – indeed, crucial – because it was the start of the celebrations for Harley's 105th anniversary. It was one long party, running from Wednesday August 27 to Monday September 1 – a party attended by around 100,000 Harley devotees.

There was something for everyone; well, something for every Harley rider. The rock 'n roll started at 4 pm on the Wednesday, even ahead of the 6 pm opening ceremony. From then on it was one long round of food, beer, music and bikes. Oh yes, and a few fireworks too.

There was a chance to view and ride the 2009 machines; you could tour the Harley site and get a good look at where the machines actually come from; there was a host of street parties; the new H-D museum was officially opened (and there were bands playing at that site too); stunt riders wowed the crowds; and there was a timetable of events just for women riders. On the Saturday morning around 8,000 bikes were ridden through the city to congregate eventually at the Summerfest Grounds. It seemed like half of Milwaukee had turned out to watch the parade go by.

The line-up of bands at the 105th was truly impressive. You can't argue with a bill that includes ZZ Top, Joan Jett and the Blackhearts, The Black Crowes, Dr John, Peter Frampton and Blue Oyster Cult. But none of those was the headliner. Harley-Davidson got it 100% right by drafting in Bruce Springsteen and The E Street Band.

Bruce and the band haven't performed a lazy gig in their lives, and their show at the Harley-Davidson Roadhouse on the Lakefront was up there with the best. Bruce believes in value for money for his fans too, and he and the guys played for more than three and half hours, performing more than 30 songs.

And what a set list! If you're a fan of The Boss it wouldn't be hard to come up with that number of songs to play to an audience of Harley riders – indeed, the problem would be deciding what to leave out. In fact the list was absolutely perfect, starting with the new – but very appropriate – Gypsy Biker, and running on through Darkness on the Edge of Town, Racing In The Street, Born To Run, and Thunder Road ... before ending the encore with their own version of Born To Be Wild. It couldn't have been more perfect, and there couldn't have been a more appreciative audience. As they say, 'Man, you should have been there'. **SM**

Money for a good cause

Throughout the celebrations, Harley's chosen charity
The Muscular Dystrophy Association gained a lot of exposure,
and everything from an anniversary Softail to a Harley-themed
Fender guitar was on offer at the charity auction on the Saturday.
In all, the staggering sum of $6,787,630 was raised for the MDA
at the event. The money was received on behalf of the MDA by
veteran comedian Jerry Lewis. Harley-Davidson has been an MDA
national sponsor for 28 years, and in that time Harley-Davidson
customers, dealers, suppliers and employees have raised more
than $65 million.

THE BIKE PARKS

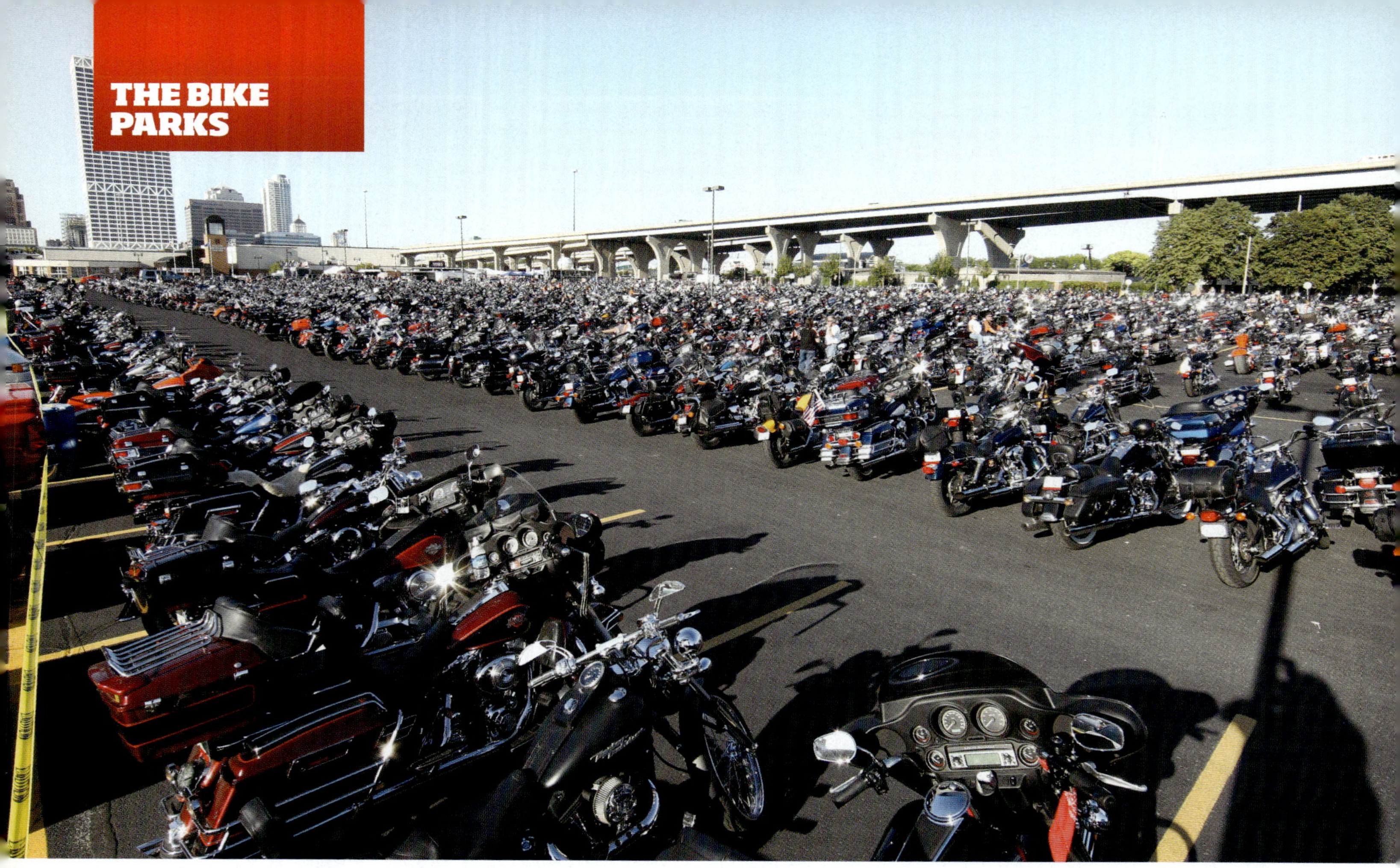

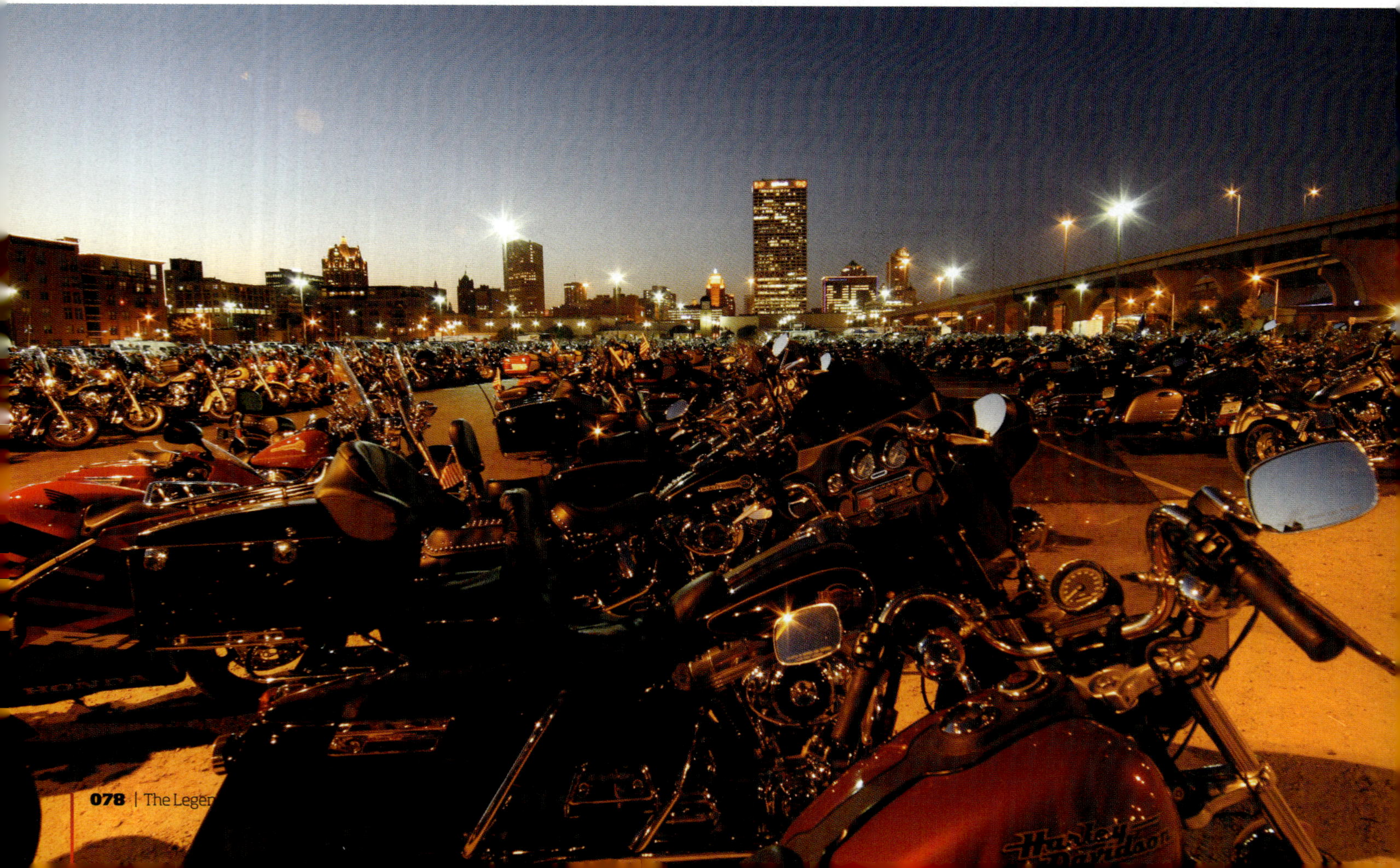

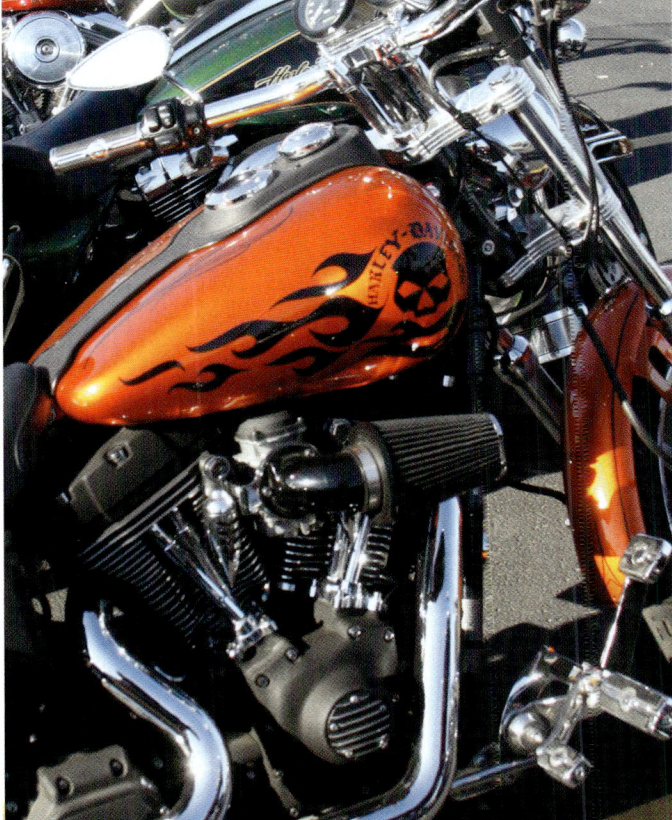

HARLEY-DAVIDSON

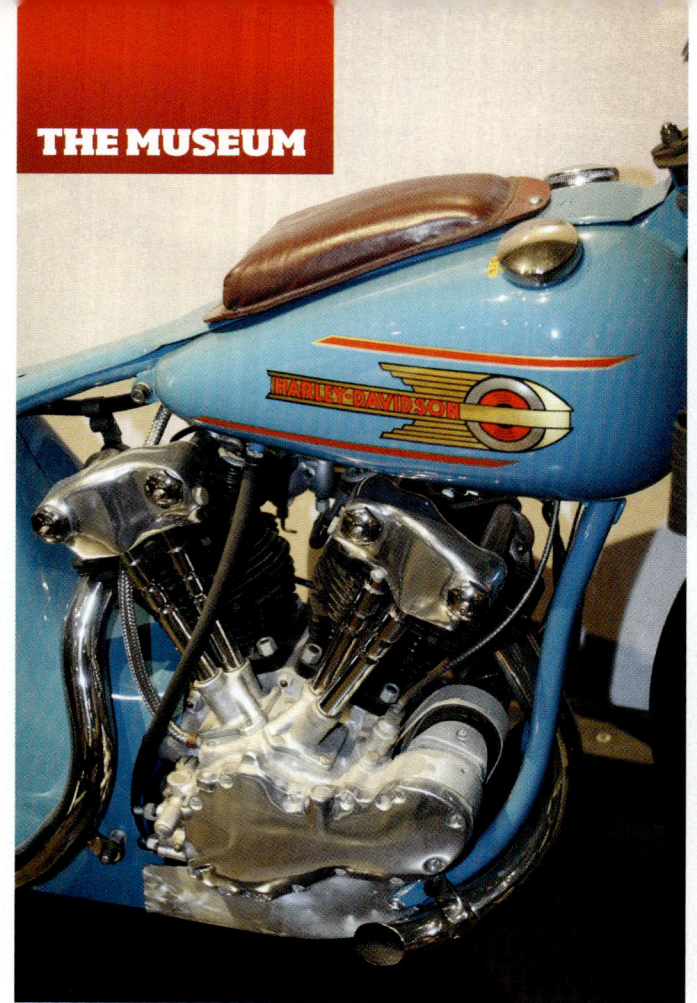

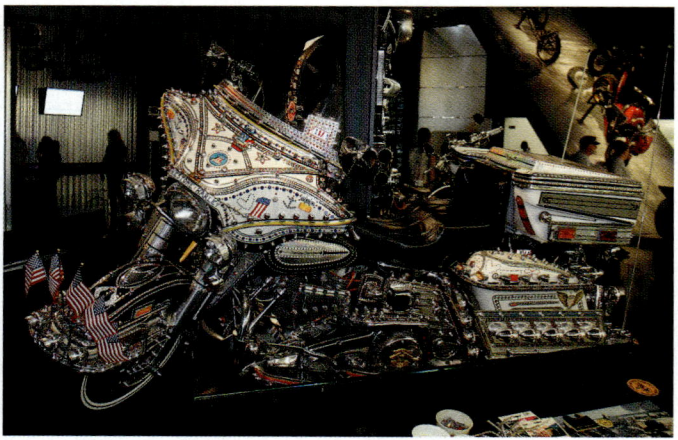

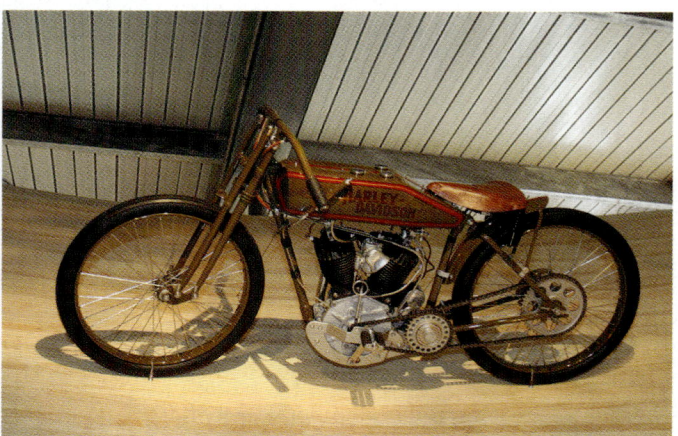

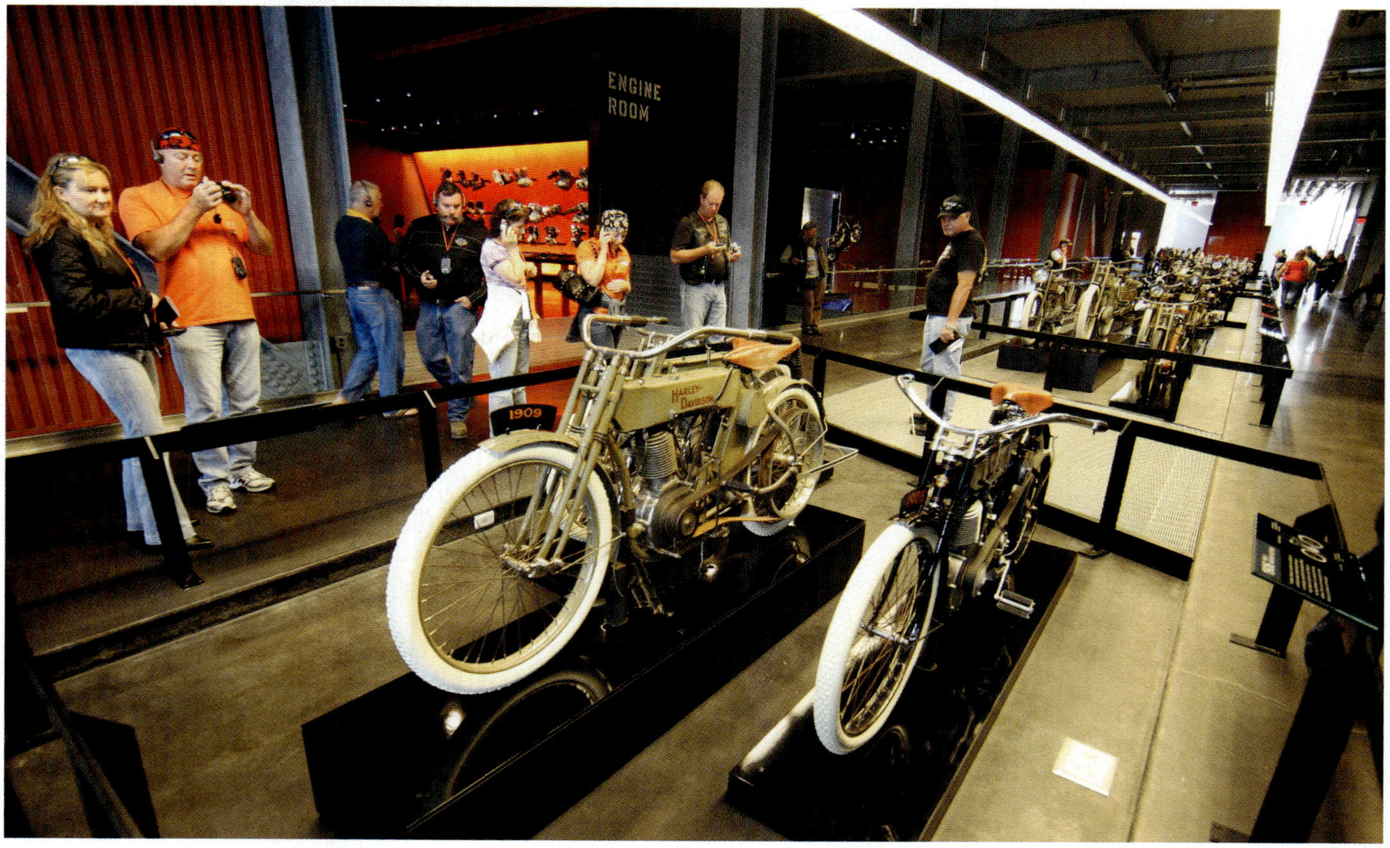
ENGINE
ROOM
1909

Harley-Davidson Museum

Harley's new museum was opened just in time for the 105th birthday celebrations, and tickets to go round it sold out long before that. Features include an extraordinary display of early board racing machines on a canted circuit, plus Joe Petrali's record-breaking Knucklehead. Also on show are a broad selection of fascinating prototypes and mock-ups, and the overhead valve V4 NOVA tourer prototype dating from the Eighties

Ron Finch Customs

To coincide with the anniversary celebrations, the Milwaukee Museum of Art put on an exhibition of bikes built by customiser Ron Finch. Ron has been building custom bikes since the late Sixties and his designs have been notable for their elaborate, baroque styling and ornate, swooping curves.

Tricks Of The Trade

The various display teams did their thing at the Henry Maier Festival Park, which became a rock arena at night. Doing wheelies and stoppies on any sort of bike takes a lot of effort, but trying it on a big tourer is wild. The Electra-Glides are the Bruce Rossmeyer formation team (Bruce owns more than a dozen H-D dealerships, and is one of the brand's biggest retailers). Police motorcycle display teams came from over the USA to show off their skills too. These guys on – and off – their Flatheads and Knuckleheads are the very rightly famous Seattle Cossacks, don't you love 'em? The guys on Buells and Sportsters are relative newcomers, Team Illconduct.

Words By: Louise Limb

BABES 'N HARLEYS:

A Post-Feminist Point-Of-View

Here's an easy task: imagine a woman and a Harley-Davidson together. What do you see? Do you imagine a scantily-clad babe with enormous breasts, pouting her lips and sticking her bum out like a porn star? Or a woman actually riding the Harley; maybe a Twenty-First century woman on a contemporary machine, or – just possibly – an early pioneer, riding her bike on unmade roads in the Twenties? Hmmm, not so easy really.

As well as being an artist and motorcycling illustrator, I also work as an art tutor – which is more than logical, I suppose. Back in the early Nineties I got talking to one of my elderly art students, Mary. She was a twinkly-eyed 82 year-old watercolourist, originally from rural Northumberland and she had been a keen motorcyclist in the 1920s. She had bombed around off-road on her friend's hefty Zenith, handling the bike like a natural extension of her horse riding

She was not unusual for her time; many girls in the post-war liberation of the 1920s wrapped their skirts around their knees, donned a warm coat and goggles if it rained, and took to two wheels. Mary's dad forbade her to ride solo on the road or go in pubs, and the dutiful daughter never did.

Tea shops catered for bikers and car drivers alike though, the latter covered in as much road grime as the former, and the camaraderie, she said, could be likened to that between long distance walkers. As Mary said, 'I was just a country girl and a tomboy. I did what I liked'.

Tomboy indeed, and quite the opposite to the scantily clad pin up babes we see draped across the latest offerings from the motorcycle manufacturers or pouting over the shiny chrome on the magazine racks on your local news stand. Sex sells, of course, and however much we like to disregard it, ordinary women, minding their own business and riding their Harleys get caught up in the transaction, at risk of being viewed as sexless heroines or smutty whores in the process.

Even the delightfully positive We Ride, the official Harley-Davidson guide for women is shot through with words like 'confidence', 'pride' and 'adversity', and that's not just over the embarrassing business of physically picking up a dropped Softail Custom. Roughly 12% of all Harley-Davidson's motorcycle sales in 2008 were to women, and the total percentage of female Harley riders is probably higher because some women's bikes are registered in their husband's name and some will be company purchases. That's still obviously way short of 51% – which is the proportion of women to men in the world – but it's an increasing number and one Harley-Davidson would dearly like to rise still further. Those who ride already will maybe shrug and wonder why the fuss, but I want to know why it's often been perceived as unusual to see ladies alone in the saddle.

So, why exactly aren't women just left alone to ride off into the Californian sunset astride their gleaming scoots? It may well go way back to a time when ordinary women couldn't inherit in their own right, couldn't have the job they wanted, cast their vote, or indeed do anything much without their husband's permission and society's approval.

For now though I'll take you back as far as 1976; I'm at my friend's house, casually listening to her talk of Greasers and Angels, soaking up tales of hapless cycle sluts and nymphomaniac mamas, righteous ol' ladies and women-only patch clubs; their membership so hard and scary both men and women fled their steely glances. Trashy fiction and 'biker exploitation' or 'biker girls' movies with 1960s lift music soundtracks pictured the hot chick packin', or an untouchable hell fox crunching the genitals of any man who crossed her path. I was scared enough of the book covers ... and the way you couldn't buy EasyRiders just any old place, even if, as a nice girl, you'd dare to.

Before I actually got to sit on a bike, I gained my image of bikers from the pulp novels of the time – of which there were many! While most of these pulp biker books described the round of runs, fights and social intercourse from a male standpoint, Mama, the sequel to Chopper: England's King Of The Angels from the New English Library, was slightly different. Written by the doubtless pseudonymous Peter Cave, it is the story of a young woman who leads the England Hells Angels. Oh really? That must have come as a surprise to them. 'Chopper may be dead but his girl lives on' the cover states; a blonde, indomitable-looking girl, with heavily made-up eyes narrowed above a king size cigarette, and with chin raised, sneers down at you. Her tidy leather jacket falls open to reveal beads strung round a white nylon polo neck circa 1972. Shot in harsh daylight, it sets the back streets of London tone – though the descriptions inside don't match, and borrow heavily from Marianne Faithfull's The Girl on a Motorcycle of 1968. 'She pulled up the gleaming chromium zipper to her throat, revelling in the sexy feel of the cool leather against her bare flesh ... it looked sexy, yet aggressive ... almost a contradictory visual statement. The overall effect of the leather was masculine, virile...' Oh dear. She'd survived gang rape and once she had the 'throbbing power of a powerful hog engine between her thighs'. Oh dear, again.

Elaine – for that, incredibly and inappropriately, was her name – was described as being in a position to assert power over a good twenty to thirty men. However, with that power came doubt, despite the comparisons to Goddess Kali: 'Together, Elaine and the Harley completed a cipher – a secret message which screamed out blatant sexuality and the power that it brings. Elaine was the picture of sexual perfection yet somehow above it ... a fantasy figure ... she was still on

Top Left: 'Sin Money Nymph' – how's that for a cover line? I wish I'd thought of that. I think Barbie must have been modeled on this girl.
Below Pulp fiction at its (sort of) best; depicting women in both dominant and submissive biker roles.

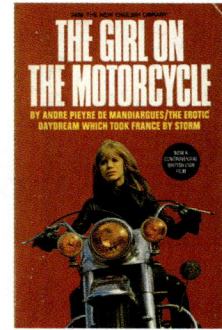
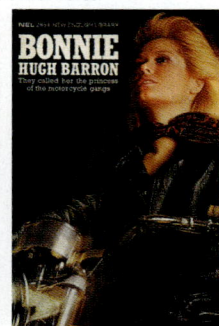

trial and she knew it … she would have to show class over and above that of any man.'

Complete hokum though this all was, there's a point lurking in there and it leads us to The Girl On A Motorcycle, a film which, despite its lavish cinematic rendering of the big Electra Glide claims to be only obliquely about women and motorcycling. The movie was released in the USA – censored – under the title Naked Under Leather. Its star, Marianne Faithfull, was one of the great faces of the Swinging Sixties, and had the perfect look for the part; apparently independent and modern, but very much a man's woman in a man's world. Her character in the film certainly does 'show class', ducking and diving between the trucks, daring to ride alone during the night without even the security of knowing that if she had the misfortune to be whisked off to 'Les Urgences' she had clean, matching undies.

French chic (left) versus British muscle (below) in the Sixties. Given the chance, I'd sooner go for a beer with Francoise Hardy.

A blonde, indomitable-looking girl, with heavily made up eyes narrowed above a king size cigarette, and with chin raised, sneers down at you

She encounters the lascivious border patrol with the candour of a small child. Why would anyone lust after her, the poor innocent, clad in this one piece lambskin-lined leather catsuit with its glittering red rhinestone zipper, handling what the petrol attendant, raised from his bed and resplendent in scruffy dressing gown, describes as 'a brute of a thing'? Of course, the Harley is her partner, constantly available, over which she has only tenuous control and which is capable of supplying her with thrills no man could hope to match. And she knows it well. Little wonder women riding motorcycles either scare men into trying to reassert control or give them a hard-on just watching the spectacle. They'd have had a shock chasing after the rider in The Girl on a Motorcycle; the actual riding was done by circuit racer Phil Read wearing a blonde wig.

Marianne Faithfull's Rebecca embodied the idea of a 1960s liberated, independently wealthy, and hedonistic woman pleasuring herself with an expensive sex toy (even if she was married to a bore and had her fun at his expense; shades of Lady Chatterley and her lover from the previous decade). And there were enough people out there who thought the formula a decent one. The style was adopted by the French chanteuse Francoise Hardy, who sang, dabbled in films and astrology, and became iconic in the way only beautiful French women seem able to be. She was pictured several times on or with motorcycles, the most famous being the leather jacket and helmet photograph on the cover on teen magazine Salut Le Copains. Even Bob Dylan was enchanted by Hardy and mentioned her in lines of poetry on his album Another Side Of Bob Dylan. Who can blame him?

Mr Zimmerman was more a Triumph man, but Brigitte Bardot liked her Harleys, famously spreading her slim legs across a custom Flathead. The mono still is famous, but you can also find video of

the encounter on Youtube, and it's well worth viewing. She's in a leather mini dress and thigh boots and is miming terribly badly. Do we care? No. Her impish pronunciation of 'Harlay Dayveed-sohn' is rather fetching, though whether she actually rode the bike or not was doubtless irrelevant to those slavering over her (of course she didn't).

Luciana Paluzzi, playing Fiona Volpe in the 007 movie Thunderball, is – surprisingly – the only Bond girl to pilot a bike (not a Harley, sadly, but a fully-faired BSA) and of course was clad in the now-predictable one-piece leather suit. Honor Blackman's Cathy Gale rode a bike in that other pioneering and stylish leather-fest, The Avengers. Diana ▶

Rigg's even sexier Emma Peel had a great line in leather catsuits but didn't need to ride a motorcycle to get the message across (the open-topped Lotus Elan messed up her hair just as much though).

By the time high psychedelia was in full swing, Janis Joplin was having herself photographed on a cool chopper with a lace paintjob for her 1973 Greatest Hits album cover. She was one of those hippie chicks who crossed over into the much heavier biker culture, and whereas Marianne Faithfull looked as if butter wouldn't melt in her mouth, you could have melted butter all over Janis – and had a queue of bikers ready and waiting to lick it off. It was symptomatic of the difference in style that Janis also used the baddest of the underground artists, Robert Crumb, for the amazing Cheap Thrills cover.

From the 1950s to the 1970s (at least), ordinary women were seen very much as passive pillion fodder; Kathy runs away from the big bully Johnny chasing her on a Triumph Speed Twin, but she's loving it really. The suggestion is that to want to ride your own bike would mean you are confused about your sexuality, or at the very least be a bit deviant.

Interviews with London Hells Angels in the underground magazine OZ in 1968 confirmed that lost young girls were much taken with the idea of playing out the role of 'Property Of'. A girl by the name of Christine describes how the 'mommas' were expected to 'pull a train', obediently making themselves available for every male biker present. A guy by the name of Levi confirms this; 'So we get down and all have a go. Too bad if she can't last the time. They have to do this before they can become a momma. Everyone has to sample the goods.' Christine goes on; 'We have a chick society to help girls ... wash their hair, clean their clothes, patch them up when they're hurt, clean the boys' bikes: Angels' girls who need help. I love being with the Angels. I've been with them two weeks. I like being 'Property Of'. I'll have a jacket with 'Property of Levi Hell's Angels' stitched on it.'

Was all this true, back then? In England? Or had they read too much Hunter S Thompson? Was it California imagined in Catford? OZ's writer probably recorded faithfully what he was told, but it's not hard to believe that the interviewees were gilding the lily a bit (or a lot) for him. It wasn't long before the mass media jumped on the 'outlaw biker outrage' bandwagon though. They'd found a new moral outrage and they loved it. What could be presented as extreme and sensationalist teen behaviour was nectar to the media who, as ever, helped shape how we see the world and the commodities we consume.

What of the biker lifestyle magazines though? That's supposed to be 'our' media. Do they merely portray women as lesser mortals, there to decorate the back of the bike and fetch the beers? Well, yes and no.

EasyRiders magazine was launched in June 1971 as an offshoot of the Jammers parts catalogue. The first issue looks very quaint today, with its cover-line boasting that the rag was aimed to be 'For The Swinging Biker', and its sissy bar designing competition. The very first thing you notice though is the lack of a cover girl, and when girls did first appear they were hardly the huge-busted southern Californian pole dancers you see today. Some of the early cover girls looked decidedly frumpy, and one or two looked as if their faces had caught fire and been put out with an old shovel. These days,

Opposite: We're all thinking 'I'd like to see you kick-start that 45 in bare feet, lady', aren't we? Hippy style from Bike magazine, contrasting with (above) Back Street Heroes much more real-world approach from the Eighties (and yup, that girl in the red top really was incredibly tall).

with its pneumatic babes and swimwear competitions, the girls too are as artificial as some of the bikes.

Which ever way you look at it, EasyRiders was also amazingly misogynistic. A lot of the jokes were savage put-downs of women, and you never knew if the readership went along with this because they were like-minded, or because EasyRiders was the bible and the readership simply accepted that that was how they ought to be thinking.

They'd have had a shock chasing after the rider in *The Girl on a Motorcycle*; the actual riding was done by circuit racer Phil Read in a blonde wig

Things were a bit different in Europe. Although not a biker lifestyle mag, Bike lead the way in being cool, and included appreciative features on choppers. They also had girls on their covers on occasion, and they tended to be loon-panted hippies, who looked (a) slightly stoned, and (b) not difficult to talk out of their knickers. They were real

women though; you could imagine them walking down the street. You could certainly imagine them shopping in real-life boutiques.

SuperBike, which was launched in 1977, wasn't a biker lifestyle magazine either, but like its sister title Custom Car, it almost always had a cover shot which featured a girl with a bike (be it a production bike, a classic, a race machine or whatever). These women were a lot glossier, the shots were taken in studios and they were professional photographic models, professionally lighted and perfectly made up. You could tell. They never looked as if they rode the bikes they were photographed with, and they would certainly never have been able to clean a fouled spark plug by the side of the road on a cold, wet night.

Everything changed though with Back Street Heroes. Launched in 1983 by Steven Myatt (the editor of this very publication), it was Europe's first true biker lifestyle magazine. BSH always had girls with bikes on the cover, but there was a crucial difference.

BSH's cover girls were real lifestyle biker girls. Partly because the magazine was launched on a budget, there was no cash for professional models or expensive studios. Steven would go up to girls at biker runs and parties and try out the age-old line; 'Can I take your photo for the cover of a magazine?' And you know what? He never once got his face slapped; though on occasion there'd be a boyfriend looking daggers at him.

His criteria, he said, was that the girl always had to look as if she belonged with the bike in question, and she also had to be the prettiest girl in the place – but not so gorgeous that a guy couldn't imagine himself walking up to her (after a couple of beers, perhaps) and trying a chat-up line. ◢

Steven had worked on both Custom Car and SuperBike previously, and though he said that he liked the idea of having girls on front covers – because the human eye is always drawn to another human face, and anyway, custom bikes are damn sexy – the pro model route wasn't going to be right for BSH. You shouldn't just write a cheque and buy in a female body; too lazy, and it told the readers that you really weren't connected with what was happening, out there on the back streets. It also helped of course that real women worked on Back Street Heroes too, but that's another story ...

This is all a far cry from the Ladies Of Harley, who today organise H.O.G. chapter events and women's garage parties, and generally operate as any other club would – from the Women's Institute to your local art club. The stereotype has WI women fragrant with lavender and neat in their twinsets – and the Ladies of Harley with rose tattoos, bandanas and chaps – while both in reality wear jeans and jumpers.

There has been no shortage of notable women Harley-Davidson riders over the past 100 years. A smattering of celebrities have been rumoured to ride, such as Tina Turner, Cher and Elizabeth Taylor – but more sensibly, one can trace a line through Harley-Davidson's history of women who have ridden across the USA, formed clubs, raced and simply done the same things as the equally outstanding male Harley riders.

'I could go places. Adventure just tingled in my blood. It made me so mad to hear that no girl should ride one'.

As early as 1915, mother Avis and daughter Effie Hotchkiss set out to ride across America on a three-speed Harley sidecar outfit. They did it just for the fun of it, and reached the Pacific in August of that year, two months after they departed Brooklyn, New York. Having arrived, they simply pointed their wheels eastwards and rode back again. They considered the outfit to be the best mode of transport for the job, and they encountered only a few difficulties – like running out of spare inner tubes in remote New Mexico (and coming up with a rolled up, cut-down blanket as a running repair).

Della Crewe from Waco, Texas, was also inspired to get out and ride. In 1915 she loaded up her 1914 Harley and sidecar, having had, at that point, a total of ten days' riding experience. She took her dog, Trouble, with her on her jaunts around America, and ran into bureaucracy when crossing State lines ... but only because some States were anxious to quarantine the mutt. Her main problem was snow, although having a sidecar helped keep out of trouble. Farmers thought her crazy when she stopped for help or shelter. Like the Hotchkiss girls, Miss Crewe had clay roads to deal with in the main; terrible, sticky surfaces which clogged the bike's wheels when it rained.

Vivian Bales, a dance instructor from Georgia, became 'The

Top: We're into kitsch korner now. Seventies porn star moustache dude with ... well, a Seventies porn star, I'd guess (and I think she's put her back out). **Right**: A very different approach from Harley Women magazine.

Enthusiast Girl' after she traded a Harley Model B single she had bought in 1926. She decided to upgrade and went for a 1929 45 twin D model, which she described as 'a real honey'. She then set off from home and rode the bike all of 5,000 miles in 78 days – at the tender age of twenty. Arthur Davidson called her 'The Georgia Peach', and though Harley-Davidson wouldn't sponsor her ride, individual dealers did support her as she rode across the States. She wrote up her journey

articulately for The Harley-Davidson Enthusiast.

Of her bike she said, 'I could go places. Adventure just tingled in my blood. It made me so mad to hear that no girl should ride one'. Vivian had lots of fun on the wet clay roads too, but had learned to ride – and to kick over a hefty 45 twin – on the sand and earth roads in Georgia. When she met President Hoover on her travels back in 1929, she was wearing one of the two white sweaters embroidered with 'The Enthusiast Girl' that Harley-Davidson gave her for her ride. When she died in 2001 at the age of 92, even after many years without a motorcycle, Vivian had her last wish – a motorcycle procession at her funeral.

Dot Robinson was a great character. She began work at her father's Harley dealership in 1912, eventually bought the business, and then moved to Detroit in the 1930s. Her speciality was winning enduro races, and tales are told of how the men could never catch her; one chasing her fruitlessly through mud and trees for two days. At the end of the race, the blokes dragged their muddy gear into the bar to hit the beers, while Dot would change and then re-appear, make-up perfect and wearing a black sheath dress and pill-box hat. Her standards of dress carried over into her contribution as founding president of The Motor Maids, which is still a force to be reckoned with in American motorcycling today. Its members are resplendent at events in neat black trousers, blue shirts, white waistcoats and their trademark white gloves.

It took three years for Dot and Linda Dugeau (another founding member) to find the fifty-one ladies who would form the charter members so that the organisation could be incorporated. Linda was one of the best off-road riders of the 1950s, and worked as a motorcycle

courier, hosting tours in undeveloped Southern California. She would think nothing of undertaking trips covering 3,500 in two weeks and had a penchant for riding on near-impassable roads in uninhabited areas of Canada.

There are now a considerable number of women's motorcycle clubs, from the Women's International Motorcycle Association to the hilariously-named Dykes On Bikes, and even a small coterie of outlaw clubs. All are conscious that they have a point to prove, even if they don't want to have to. It doesn't take too much reading on club websites to find quotes like this one of Dot Robinson, 'She proved that you can be a lady, still compete with the men and not be a man-hater', or 'We would ride on the back with boyfriends or husbands, but some of us were tomboys and rode dirt bikes', as The Women In The Wind site observes. Refreshingly, Britain's Motorcycle Action Group has always embraced jumpers and jeans on either gender, and neither patronises the ladies nor makes a special case for women on motorcycles. Their members are all just bikers, pure and simple.

It is, however, the Motorcycle Queen of Miami to whom we really do owe our respect. Bessie Stringfield didn't just have to deal with prejudice against her as a woman. She also had to cope with vicious racism. She was raised by her adoptive Irish mother after she was orphaned at the age of five, and her Catholic faith in 'The Man Upstairs' carried her over a number of setbacks which would have floored most of us. She completed rigorous training to serve in the US Army as a civilian motorcycle despatch rider in World War Two, and broke down barriers both for women and for African-American motorcyclists. Her first bike was a 1928 Indian Scout bought when she was just sixteen. She claimed Jesus taught her to ride and she took Him with her up front, alongside the Indian-face horn. He went on to accompany her on her following twenty-seven Harleys.

'To me,' she said, 'A Harley is the only motorcycle ever made'. As a black person she often couldn't find a place to sleep on her journeys through the forty-eight lower States, making do with filling stations, resting her feet on the rear footrests and using her jacket as a pillow across the handlebars. Amongst other racial abuse, Bessie was once run off the road by a man in a pickup truck, but she shrugged off such incidents as her 'ups and downs'. Finding fame through stunt and trick riding, it is said she once won a flat track race disguised as a man, but when she took off her helmet she was denied the prize money. She rode bikes for over sixty years, claiming that if she stopped riding she'd not live long. Once she quit, she didn't, and she died in 1993 at the age of 82.

I suspect that a woman will always be conscious as she rides her Harley-Davidson that she might be the object of curiosity, and that men will always be slightly confused by her. She just needs to take advantage of the power that conveys and watch out as one website observes, that whatever happens she doesn't fall into the ultimate trap and 'ride like a girl'.

CHOP AGAINST THE CLOCK

The guys from Hawg Haven build a bobber for Carole Nash – with one eye on the clock

This is a curious occurrence; an insurance company building a custom bike. It's not what you expect, is it? Insurance companies … well, they insure your bike; they don't build it for you.

The key fact here though is that we're talking about Carole Nash, and that business has always been rather different from the common run of insurance companies. Put it this way; think of any other bike insurance company, any at all, and ask yourself if it has a 'face' – a personality. The answer's no, isn't it? Carole Nash, in contrast, has always had a personality – friendly, reliable, and definitely pro-biking.

For years the company has always had a big stand at the International Motorcycle Show, held at the NEC every November. If you want to rendezvous with mates you say 'I'll see you at the Carole Nash stand at 12 o'clock'. Which you'd do, and then you head for the bar. And they've often had custom bikes on the stand, many of which they've commissioned themselves. At the last show things were just a little bit different …

Hawg Haven is a custom bike building business, who you can find out in the badlands of Norfolk. Run by Jon Quantrell and Terry Clarke, they're a high profile operation, and have recently built bikes for television cooks The Hairy Bikers and for long-distance rider Charlie Boorman.

The notion was a simple one – well, simple but mad. With no preparatory work done before, four Hawg Haven guys were going to start the show with a pile of bits and pieces, and build a show-standard custom bike, ready to run, before the exhibition closed. It was to take place in a special

'Carole Nash Construct' area, which had to be set well aside from the visitors for safety's sake – in a glass and aluminium chequer plate box - so the quartet were virtually locked in for the duration.

It had been agreed that they would create an old school bobber, and with a cavalier disregard for Her Majesty's written English, they called it The Carole Nash Old Skool Bobber. The ingredients were a stock-shape Santee frame and a 1540 cc Revtech motor, but those aside, most everything else was going to be created in front of the show's 150,000 visitors.

Carole Nash has got form of course when it comes to surprising the NEC crowds with truly startling custom bikes. More than a decade ago the company brought three Arlen Ness bikes – Smoothness, Aluminess and Antiqueness – over from the States to grace the stand. There was a point to be made; namely, that insurance cover and custom machines can make sense together. Carole Nash was saying that the company understand the investment that goes into a custom bike, and that one of their agreed valuation policies can protect your precious metal if something goes wrong.

But back to the NEC build-up. Work started at 9am on November 28 2008 as the show opened to the public, and the first job was modifying the frame to suit the builders' vision. By Monday the gleaming engine was sitting in the now-goosenecked and hard-tailed frame, and things were looking good. This wasn't a case of just bolting after-market parts on, oh no; many components were fabricated on the stand from scratch, and many others – such as the petrol tank – were modified and re-worked. Even the wheels were built up on site.

By Tuesday afternoon the bike had been painted and the motor was sitting in a frame which was now a very fetching shade of blue, and the old-style springers were being bolted on. The following day it became clear that there was a problem though. The lovely shiny tank wasn't right. Someone had misjudged the set-up and the 'bars were hitting the front of tank on full lock. Whoops. As they say at this sort of point, 'back to the drawing board' – or, in the English vernacular, 'Oh sh*t'. On a more positive

THE SPEC

Frame: Santee
Engine: 88 ci/1450 cc Revtech V-twin
Gearbox: Revtech 5-speed Secondary drive: BDL 3-inch open belt
Wheels: 16-inch chrome
Exhaust: Bespoke stainless steel, 2-into-1 hi-level
Paint: Carole Nash's blue and green colours
Value: £30,000

note, the primary drive was in place and all the hoses had been fitted.

Thursday was the day to make the exhaust, and make sense of the wiring harness, and neither task presented any worries. The problem with the tank was solved, and it was time to look forward to …

Everything else happened in a gratifying rush on Friday and Saturday, and then Sunday was The Big Day. The starter motor was bolted in, a couple of quarts of engine were poured in, and yes, the motor fired. Now, you're not really supposed to crack up internal combustion engines in enclosed spaces – let alone 1450 cc monsters, but hey, they've got to catch you before they can stop you. And it sounded great. Sighs of relief all round were drowned out by the crackle.

After all of 400 man hours Jon and Terry were ready to hand the keys over to Rebecca Donohue, Carole Nash's Head of Marketing. Job done, eh? Not quite; one last thing to do … the guys went off for a beer. Meanwhile, the rest of us stood back to admire the Carole Nash Old Skool Bobber. Nice, eh?

To view a blog of the build-up go to *http://www.carolenash.com/ insidebikes/carole-nash-construct-blog-archive*

CAROLE NASH

Visit **www.carolenash.com** or call **0800 988 0261**

It would be too terrible a pun to say that the custom Harley has never stood still – but you know what I mean. In the way that you can look at a piece of furniture or a painting and date it by its style, you can do just that with a custom bike.

If I showed you a photo of a Fifties bobber, you'd know exactly what you were looking at. If I showed you an early Seventies chopper with a kite-shaped tank and a set of exhausts which were a hazard to low-flying aircraft, then again you'd be able to put a date to it unhesitatingly.

Matters get a bit more curious as you get into the twenty-first century, though. There are so many different styles of custom H-D being built that it's rather more complex. Over the next few pages we've brought together a whole wide mix of styles – some aggressively modern, some reassuringly retro – in a round-up of what's happening right now. This isn't everything that's about, needless to say; we'd need a thousand pages to do that. For now though, here's just a taste.

So, what's your preference? Which bike would you like to see in front of your house? Me? I really can't decide …

JAKE'S RETRO PAN

Words & photos: Steve Kelly

Heavily tattooed and pierced, sinewy and lean, Jake Smith is something of an anomaly. For starters, how many Jewish skinheads have you ever come across? Then again, how many skinheads are avid potters? As in, with clay and a potting wheel. I think the answer to both is none. Let's just say, Jake marches to his own drum and leave it at that.

An extremely young Jake showed up at Exile Cycles one day and begged Russell Mitchell to hire him. He claimed that he would do absolutely anything, and was even willing to work for free, if that was what it would take to get a Doc Martin boot in the door. Russell was impressed by Jake's passion and perseverance, so eventually he was hired to assist in the packing department. This was not quite what he was looking for, but he was happy to start at the bottom.

Jake would show up early each morning, work hard at boxing and shipping products all day, then hang around after work in his own time, trying to figure out how things were machined, or how they were put together. It wasn't long before Jake had proved that he had a natural aptitude for all things mechanical, so Russell took him under his wing, thus Jake's progression through the Exile ranks began.

By the time Jake left Exile to set up his own custom motorcycle shop – named Ultra Violence – he had been head mechanic for four years. However, he had gleaned more than technical ability from Russell – he had witnessed the power of advertising and promotion from the self-proclaimed media whore. These were tools that he would need if his fledgling company was to succeed.

Prior to starting Ultra Violence, Jake already had five Discovery Channel Biker Build-off programmes under his belt. These gave him confidence, and increased the recognition factor, as his face was already well known throughout the industry. As his myspace page proudly proclaims: 'I'm ready to create you an amazing custom motorcycle, either from an all aftermarket build, or to create you a stock Harley, that is anything but stock.'

This 1995 pseudo-Panhead project started life as a Harley-Davidson Heritage Nostalgia. It had done the rounds for almost five years before it ended up at Jake's workshop in North Hollywood. It was a common enough tale; a guy had bought it for his wife as a Christmas present, but he soon discovered that though he tried very hard, with massive work commitments, he just didn't have the time to complete the project himself. It was passed from shop to shop and builder to builder, and they lost interest in the bike. Eventually they found Jake, a man who was so interested and enthusiastic about the metamorphosis from stock Harley-Davidson Heritage Nostalgia into a customer's Pan of dreams, that he was able to complete all the work that others could not in just a couple of months.

While the project was with Matt Hotch, of Hot Match Custom Cycles, he got as far as shaving .030 mm off the heads to increase the compression ratio, and painstakingly stripped the factory wrinkle paint from the engine. Then he added gloss black to the cylinders to give the bike its authentic look. It's the Panhead rocker covers and generator-style cam cover that Jake fitted that give the motor, and whole motorcycle, its truly distinctive vintage look though.

The retro feel was further bolstered by the use of a set of Paughco springers. Jake also elected to use a tank-shift mechanism to give the right feel to the project. He removed the front master cylinder, preferring the rear master cylinder to operate both front and back brakes, leaving the handlebars less cluttered in the process. That's a little trick he had picked up while working at Exile.

The swing arm has been extensively reworked by Jake, so that the rear aftermarket copy vintage fender could be mounted

symmetrically. It took many hours of painstaking graft to get that right, but he believes that it was worth it in the end. Jake tailor-made the handlebars, custom shifter arm, exhaust pipes and headlight bracket. He also cannibalised three different primary belt drives to get the best look for this hybrid ride. Tony Marcus laid down the Hollywood Green paintwork, which is an original Harley-Davidson colour dating back to the mid 1930s. Jake then took the metalwork to Te & Thick of Venice CA, who incorporated the Sanskrit symbols.

Being the modest man that he is, Jake would like to thank the rest of his Ultra Violence crew; Blake Schosler, Paul Kirk, Kimarra Stefanski, Keith Smith, Jeff Teideken and Wyoming Dave for getting the bike finished and on the road.

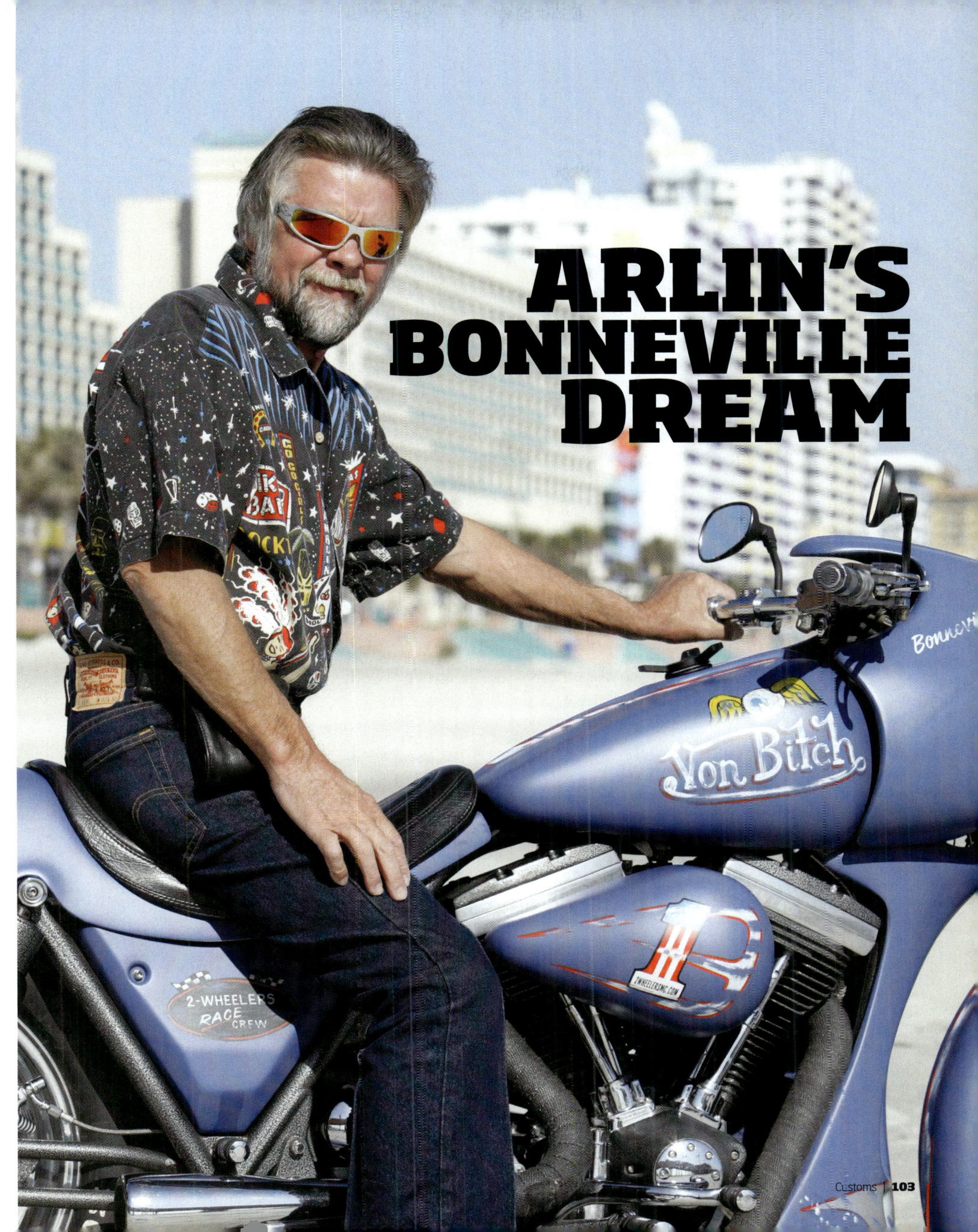

ARLIN'S
BONNEVILLE
DREAM

The Bonneville salt flats are the bed of a once massive lake; the flats are composed mainly of potash salts, ranging in thickness from less than one inch to around six feet, and cover 159 square miles. The flats extend some nine miles along US Highways 40 and 50 and the Western Pacific Railroad. Early attempts to promote automobile racing failed until 1925, when Ab Jenkins drove his Studebaker across the flats ten minutes faster than a special excursion train he was racing. Since that time, the Bonneville Salt Flats have attracted racers from throughout the world, chasing numerous land speed records. The annual Speed Week festival is held when the weather over the flats puts them at their best for racing. Magically, each rainfall erases the tyre marks and re-flattens the densely packed salt.

During the Fifties and Sixties the salt flats became a motor sports mecca – perhaps most famous for special race cars that have achieved speeds in excess of 600mph, but almost equally renowned for motorcycle speed freaks. Competing bikers from around the globe now meet annually at the salt flats to enter the only AMA-sanctioned land- speed race held solely for motorcycles.

Denis Manning has been chasing land speed records with numerous motorcycles for more than three decades. In September 2006, his BUB 7 Streamliner captured the ultimate goal when it set the new absolute motorcycle land speed record. Rider Chris Carr piloted BUB 7 to an average, both-way speed, of 350.885mph.

They say that everything old becomes new again, a time worn adage that's especially true when it comes to custom Harley-Davidson V-twin motorcycles. Mike Corbin created the fairing, front frame rail cowling and seat/tail unit for Arlin's salt flats creation; a setup which, coupled with Arlin's extensive reworking of an eighty cubic inch Evolution motor, has seen Arlin take top honours in his class … but only for beer drinking. Yards of carefully sculptured fibreglass do the trick for some salt flats racers, but Arlin's street rider credentials took him in a different direction. He likes to be able to see a bike's components, rather than have them completely sheathed, even if that brings a penalty in terms of reduced top speed.

For decades, you were more likely to see a modified British bike than an American Harley-Davidson racer wearing a full fender. That was until Corbin noticed a similar design characteristic between the svelte, sculpted lines of the Bonneville race bikes and vintage World War II Warbird fighter planes. To meld the two classic designs, Corbin created the Warbird kit that graces Arlin's bike. It's a custom bodywork kit that can be used to transform an ordinary looking Harley-Davidson FXR into a vision of what a modern day streetfighter can be, and if you think about it, if a Panhead can set a land speed record of 161mph, what can an Evolution engine achieve?

If you look closely at Arlin's paintwork you will find 1970 emblazoned on it. This is when Arlin set up his fledgling motorcycle shop in Denver, Colorado. The faux antique paint job catches a lot of attention when the bike is parked on Sturgis or Daytona's Main Street in front of Arlin's other custom bike shops. Old School hotrod enthusiasts love the look of the bike, kids point and stare, and the masses give it more than a passing glance. Racers don't have much in the way of chrome, so Arlin stripped the primary and rocker boxes and chassis and shipped them over to Taint Paint for complementary powder coating. The instant patina is what people really love about the bike, but I find it hard to understand how some bikers can really think that this bike really was raced in Bonneville back in 1970, not

least because the Evo engine wasn't released until 1982! Let me be 100% clear about this, it has never been ridden at Bonneville – only in Arlin's beer-addled dreams…

Perhaps Arlin had been reading the book his friend Keith Ball released. 'How to Build a Bonneville Salt Flats Motorcycle', documents the construction of the World's Fastest Panhead. Arlin bought a mountain of Miller Lite, then took an entire week off work to complete this project. While some dream of getting land speed records, others keep off the beer long enough to do it.

The 2009 BUB Motorcycle Speed Trials will once again offer the opportunity to have a shot at glory, with a 'Run What You Brung' style of event. The event is currently scheduled to run from September 2nd through 7th. If you get the chance to go, one of the best places to watch the spectacle is beside the five-mile point, where the racers scream past with their throttles wide open. And who knows, Arlin might even be there, a beer in hand.

CHICA'S ULA SUPER-6

Chica Custom Cycles are located in Huntington Beach, California. They specialise in the old school look while using today's latest technology. Over the years Chica has featured in, and graced the covers of, motorcycle magazines around the globe. His attention to fine detail has earned him a reputation as one of the world's top custom bike builders.

A bike from Chica is completely one off, with each machine being constructed to the customer's needs and stature as well as style. Typically a 'standard' Chica custom starts at around $40,000 and a 'full' custom starts at $45,000. This WLA-inspired ride is a distinct diversion in style from the custom master, though.

Chica started with a 1937 Harley-Davidson UL Flathead motorcycle, one of the innovative models that Harley offered as the company made its big comeback from the doldrums after the Great Depression. Flatheads were modernised by Harley-Davidson in 1937 with the adoption of a recirculation oiling system, a system that had been introduced to great affect on the Knucklehead the year before. The UL's crankpin was also enlarged, the connecting rods were strengthened, and the flywheels increased in size. In an effort to rationalise production, Harley also changed the bore size to that of the OVH 61, and the stroke to that of the 80.

Instead of overhead valves, Flathead Harley-Davidson engines have valves that run alongside the engine and open upwards into

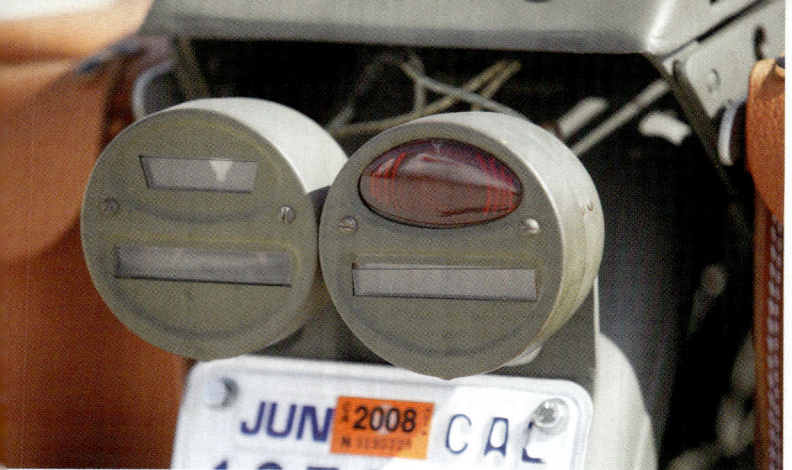

the chamber beside the combustion chamber. The advantage of this design is simplicity; there are no pushrods or rocker arms, thus the head is straightforward to cast. The 45 cubic inch version (the most commonly found variety today) produces 22 horsepower from its 742cc. Although stunningly reliable, the Flathead engine is not particularly efficient, especially in comparison to overhead valve designs, but the motor offers reliability rather than power output.

Based upon an existing WLD civilian model, the WLA 45 solo motorcycle was produced to army specifications during WWII. Regarding Harley's lettering, W stands for the family of motorcycle, L equates to high compression and A, of course, stands for army. WLAs produced after Pearl Harbour, regardless of the actual year, were given serial numbers indicating 1942 production. Thus wartime machines became known collectively as 42WLAs. Although the model designation suggests high compression, the motor was available in several compression ratio ratings. For reliability, the army opted for a medium-compression ratio of 5:1, which is, by today's standards rather low, but it did enable the WLA to run on poor-quality 74-octane fuel.

WLA motorcycles spanned Harley's history from 1940 to 1945 and then 1949 through 1952 as the US Army 45 Solo. From 1939 until 1940 Harley-Davidson produced the UA US Army 74 Flathead, and sandwiched somewhere between, the UL model Harleys ran for eleven years from 1937 to 1948 with a 74-inch (1,200cc) lump.

That is why Chica chose this model for his latest project. He then selected an even earlier frame; a 1935 model V hardtail (the V model Harley-Davidson would become the U in 1937). He then added a Baker gearbox case, upgrading Harley-Davidson's four gears for six. He has then cleverly used Harley-Davidson's own model lettering designation system to come up with the name ULA Super-6 for this motorcycle.

Chica's wartime rendition comes with modified mudguards that have the skirts cut away, enabling such a motorcycle to run across open ground with reduced mud clogging. The bike also benefits from a set of blackout head and taillights, a heavy-duty rack suitable for an army issue radio, ammo box, and a skid plate to protect the underside of the engine. The air cleaner is an oil bath type, which originated for use on tractors and other vehicles used in dusty environments. This type of cleaner allowed army bikes to work reliably even when crashing along dusty tracks. Oil bath cleaners only require the addition of standard motor oil rather than replaceable filters.

The UL model Harley replaced ammeter and oil pressure gauges with red and green lamps; on what we have all come to call a Cat Eye centre dash. Chica's machine also comes with a VL model springer front end (all WLA model bikes came with springer front suspension as Harley-Davidson did not adopt telescopic forks until well after the war). The rear wheel has no suspension at all, and of course that's where nickname 'hard tail' originated.

So, Chica's ride is no restoration project but an almost complete new build, in fact, many of the parts are from modern-day custom catalogues. That said though, the bike wonderfully demonstrates that, with the most careful selection of parts, you can build a stunning ride that will fool most of the bike aficionados most of the time.

JERRY'S BAGGER

Jerry Covington has something of an illustrious past, he has been building custom motorcycles for the past 38 years, and in that time he has built just about every type of custom motorcycle conceivable. So, it was no surprise to recently find that he had been tinkering with a 2008 Street Glide.

In between building bobbers, pro street customs, lowriders, trikes and rigid choppers, Jerry has somehow managed to find the time to run a successful business – Covington's Cycle City in Oklahoma – and to build a number of bagger-based customs. On this occasion though, the bike is more of a test bed for CCC's product development, than a bespoke ride.

Jerry's business is one of the few American custom bike shops to be weathering the economic downturn well. Having a loyal customer base helps, but Jerry saw the dip in the market coming about two years before it bit, and that gave him the breathing space needed to develop a large number of custom bagger parts, many of which you can find on this motorcycle. Compared to custom motorcycle sale opportunities, stock H-D sales are huge, and the American bagger community truly vast. Even with Harley-Davidson substantially backing off from the ▶

400,000-motorcycle production target that they set themselves for 2009, I'm sure you can see the logic behind this move. Jerry was savvy enough to see a gap in this potentially lucrative market, many others have since followed, but as the saying goes, the early bird catches the worm.

Founded in 1992 as a natural progression of Jerry's lifelong love of motorcycles, Covington's Cycle City is a real family affair. Jerry is helped by his sons David, Dusty, Peewee and Cameron on the shop floor, and his unflappable wife Kathleen runs the back office, taking care of all the administration, procurement, and bill paying, as well as the payroll. In total, Covington's has a full time staff of 18 employees. Jerry has taught the boys the craft of metal fabrication and bike building well. David, for example, has been taking many of the top American custom bike shows by storm with machines such as Lucifer II, a truly jaw-dropping high dollar ride.

One of the first things that you notice about this denim blue and silver leaf pin striped Street Glide, is the stock Harley-Davidson fairing that has been fitted with a Klock tinted and flared windshield. There is simply nothing else like it on the market. Covington's have been fitting and selling these unique windshields ever since their inception. They love the way they look, but more importantly, they enjoy the enhanced riding experience. Klock's streamlined design was developed in a wind tunnel to reduce buffeting, then proven on Bonneville's salt flats.

Next your eyes will be drawn to the unique looking, gleaming, custom fork slider covers, oddly called 'fork bells' (there is no getting away from it, American English has little in common to the Queen's!). Study the front end for a little longer and you will notice the highly detailed axle spacers and axle end covers that Jerry has designed to smarten up Harley's drab offerings. The whole bike bristles with innovative dress-up Covington parts. Check out the fluted master cylinder top plates, the brake pedal, the shifter pegs, floor board re-locators, passenger pegs, speaker grills and the Derby cover.

Jerry didn't stop there though. He went on to create matching saddlebag latch covers, licence plate frame, centre dash insert and the great looking Panhead-style valve covers, and a whole host of other goodies – oh yes, and the deliberately understated paintwork.

The stock 96-inch Twin-Cam now boasts a Bassani (true dual) high-performance exhausts with CCC fluted billet aluminium exhaust tips, a Terry Components fuel management system, and those beautiful Pan style covers. Jerry elected to fit a set of Covington's Dillinger wheels to further demonstrate what can be achieved with a little extra cash and effort. The front is a 21-inch, and the rear 18-inch. To bring the Street Glide to a controlled stop, Jerry used Wilwood brake callipers – a company that has more than three decades of experience.

Another innovative business idea that Jerry came up with was to offer free fitting of these components during major bike rallies such as Laughlin and Daytona Bike Week. Sons David and Dusty were working all the hours to keep up with demand when I stopped by the Covington booth during the River Run, demonstrating Jerry's business acumen once again. All of the Covington Cycle City bagger parts mentioned are available in a number of finishes that include chrome, black, and diamond cut edged. Contact Covington's Cycle City for more information (they are more than happy to ship worldwide).

TRASK'S V-ROD

Nick Trask, the owner of this incredibly swift matt-black V-Rod, has done a great deal more than just bolt a turbo kit on to his ride. He is in fact the designer, developer and driving force behind the company that makes those same turbo kits, which enable all and sundry to enjoy the lag-free adrenaline rush that can be delivered simply by the twist of the wrist.

Trask Performance began over a decade ago in Nick's humble garage in Bay of Islands, New Zealand. The initial concept was to start a performance centre specialising in Dyno tuning and turbo systems, but right from the off Nick's objective was to be more than that. He set himself the goal of becoming the very best.

Unfortunately, he quickly discovered that due to a lack of available parts it was next to impossible to run such a business from New Zealand. Undeterred, and determined to succeed, he rolled life's dice and moved to America.

As is true of anything worth having, it has taken time, resilience and lots and lots of hard work to get the company off the ground. Today, Nick is surrounded with a team of handpicked, highly proficient and dedicated technicians. That is an investment which has really paid dividends, and has undoubtedly contributed to the success and ever-growing reputation of Trask Performance – not only near their base in Phoenix Arizona, or indeed just across America; Trask Performance is now branching out worldwide with the introduction of the Trask Turbo System.

When I met Nick he told me that his mission was to continually improve his products and services, but equally importantly to stand 100% behind the work performed by Trask Performance. I asked Nick why his customers opted to fit a turbo to their Harleys, and he replied, saying, 'Why do people ride and drive over 100mph when the sign says 65?' The answer is … simply for the thrill of it.

Having tested Nick's turbo V-Rod, I now understand that correctly fitted and set-up, turbocharging is a breathtaking way to produce ▸

smooth, reliable horsepower. The power that is always there, just waiting for that twist of the throttle. Turbocharged engines revolve around one central idea; and that is boost. Boost is defined as the increase in manifold pressure above atmospheric pressure, so boost is the gauge measurement, meaning that the higher the boost, the more air will be forced to the engine, which in turn equates to extra horsepower. A Trask turbo typically achieves a staggering 50% horsepower increase.

There are seven basic components to a turbocharger kit:

1. An exhaust manifold that holds the turbocharger and mounts it to the motor, and directs the exhaust gases from the exhaust ports to the turbo charger inlet.

2. A down pipe that is connected to the side of the turbine housing, which lets out the spent gas through the exhaust.

3. An intercooler, which is simply a giant heat exchanger that cools the temperature of the charged air (though Nick's Stage One kit does not use an intercooler).

4. A blow-off valve, which helps to prevent compressor surge (this is the part that gives a turbo-powered vehicle its distinctive and impressive hissing sound).

5. A high-pressure fuel pump to supply the necessary fuel, which works in conjunction with a boost-sensing regulator that feeds the injections with extra fuel under boost conditions in a linear rate.

6. A waste gate, which bypasses the exhaust to control boost pressure. This maintains the turbo charger's shaft speed by opening and closing. When it opens, exhaust gases leave via the down tube and exhaust, slowing the shaft, and then when closed, the exhaust gases increase shaft speed by spooling the turbine giving you the desired boost.

7. The final component of the kit is of course the turbo itself.

You'd swear that Nick really does have engine oil running through his veins. He is the archetypal biker mechanic. Trask Performance-engineered Harleys have won more horsepower shootouts than any other builder in the USA. Their turbo FXR even smoked a nitrous-equipped Hayabusa in Tampa Florida with an 8.90 second pass at 158mph. There is no doubt in my mind that Nick really can make your Harley run stronger and smoother than you ever thought possible. I'm also convinced that turbocharging is the most cost effective way to produce rider-friendly, smooth usable power, as there are minimal drive train upgrades required. In addition, the reliability of the stock Harley-Davidson engine is retained until boost is applied.

All this means that you could ride around all day without getting in the boost zone, so fuel economy is not compromised either. Whether you have a bagger, Dyna, Softail Sportster or even a Harley-powered trike, Nick's the man to see if you want to blow away a few cobwebs.

SHINYA'S ZERO

Like many of us, even as a young boy, **Shinya Kimura** wanted to be different from the rest of his friends. To help achieve this he customised his pushbike so that he would stand out from the crowd, and in so doing, started something that was to become a life-long obsession – the quest for the ultimate form.

In 1992, Shinya quit his post as chief mechanic at one of Japan's leading motorcycle manufacturers to set up his own custom motorcycle company, Chabott Engineering, in Okazaki City. The following year Shinya changed the company name to Zero Engineering and recruited a team of five mechanics. Over the next decade or so, Zero manufactured over 200 complete custom motorcycles. The bikes that came out of the Okazaki workshop made the engine, typically an older model H-D lump such as a Knucklehead, the prominent feature. This style of custom fired the imagination of Japanese bikers, catapulting Shinya into the limelight.

The no-frills, retro-chic machines that Shinya creates are rolling works of art. He uses an eclectic selection of parts from a wide ranging source. Some come from the scrap heap or junk yard; others from vintage Harley-Davidsons. Shinya seems to craft his bikes in such a way as to bring out the inner beauty of the raw materials. In an ultra-modern world, it's refreshing to see something with patina, worn metal and muted paint schemes. All of this was a far cry from the gaudy-looking style of bike that was dominating the American custom bike scene at the time.

So how on earth did Shinya and Zero Engineering end up in America? Simple, America is still the ultimate land of opportunity. So, with a letter of recommendation from Brad Pitt, who owned three Zero bikes at the time, Shinya submitted his Green Card application to the US authorities, and was successful.

Going full circle, Shinya set up Chabott

Engineering in Azusa, California. While still working as Zero Engineering's chief designer, with a six-strong team of mechanics in Okazaki realising his visions, Shinya also began to build alone too. Many of Shinya's designs are based around themes from nature, which he frequently bestows with outlandish names such as Peanut Fighter or Frozen Lily (one of my all time favourite Zero Engineering bikes). Despite the cost of a Shinya Kimura bike, there is a rolling four-year waiting list.

Free from Japanese regulations about insurance and custom bike registration hassles, Shinya's work has been able to blossom, especially as Americans are happy to lavish money on themselves, thinking nothing of rewarding themselves for hard work with a big purchase. Back in Japan the mindset is different, people feel guilty about such activities, thinking money should be saved for their children.

Shinya's big break came in 2001, when a book showcasing 34 of his iconic motorcycles was released. The English language book, Zero Chopper Spirit: Samurai Bikes from the East, generated a huge degree of interest from around the world. E-mails, letters, and telephone calls from magazine editors from all over the globe filled Shinya's days. He started entering his bikes in custom shows, and was amazed by the response. Bikers wanted to meet him, shake his hand and take photographs, oh, so many photographs! All of which was totally different from Japan, where bikers studied his machines quietly from a distance.

This is where the Shinya Kimura/Zero Engineering story becomes a little hazy, and is hard to nail down the facts. I do know that Zero moved to Las Vegas, and someone came up with the idea of producing production custom machines to a Zero-style formula: machines such as this tasteful Evolution-based Kimono, seen here with Zero's current head honcho Hiro Sasaki. Shinya left Zero back in 2006, to form Chabott Engineering in Azusa. Chabott means bantam rooster in Japanese, but to Shinya it means Back to Basics. So for a second time, he travelled full circle.

Although I do not know for certain, I would hazard a guess as to why Shinya chose to leave Zero. Could it be as simple as the oxymoron that is the thought of a production custom bike? Kimono, just like all the other models currently produced by Zero Engineering Las Vegas, is a sweet enough looking ride, but production bikes have to compromise, they have to conform to strict rules, such as having mirrors and indicators, which waters down the original ethos.

With the rebirth of Chabott Engineering under Shinya's direction, the continued exploration of metal and rubber will once again run free in new and different ways. Not merely in the construction of custom motorcycles, but in the creation of functional art by infusing his philosophy and aesthetic values into totally unique designs; this will also keep alive the legacy that is Zero Style, and allow savvy bikers to stand out from the masses.

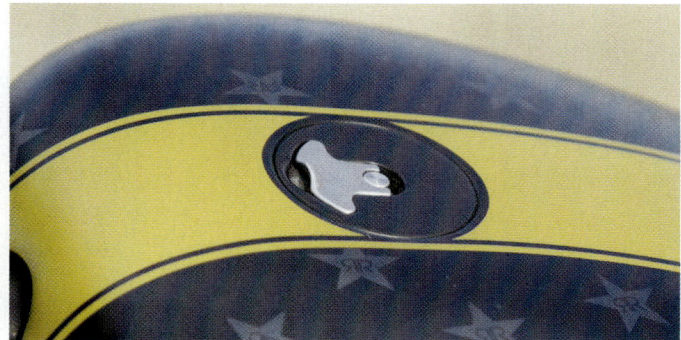

THE ROCKSTAR

Russell Mitchell and his Exile crew first met the Rockstar Energy Drink guys during the Sturgis Motorcycle Rally, back in 2005. They immediately hit it off, and enjoyed a combined week-long reign of terror in the notoriously raucous, Full Throttle Saloon (aka The World's Largest Biker Bar). Russell renamed Rockstar's main protagonists Craig and Jordan 'Bill and Ted' – you will instantly understand why if you ever get to meet them. Russell also became friends with another of Rockstar's key players, Kelso, a man who was to later kindly facilitate Exile's involvement in some very exclusive Hollywood parties at the Rockstar mansion, and also supplied them with a hospitality box at the aptly named, extreme action sports 'X' games.

It soon became clear that Exile and Rockstar had very similar company sensibilities, and it seemed only logical for Rockstar to get behind Exile with a sponsorship deal. A plan was hatched that entailed Exile developing the definitive Rockstar Bike, and that is how this beautiful satin black beast came to be created.

The first step of the project was for Russell to put together an artist's rendition that encapsulated his idea of the ultimate Rockstar machine. Once this was complete, he sent the artwork to Rockstar's Corporate Management for their input. Now, as I'm sure you can imagine, Corporate Management types take their own sweet time making up their minds. Months and months passed, causing Russell untold anxiety. As the suits, really were taking forever, Russell just went ahead and built the bike the way he wanted it to look. All of which means that Rockstar have been given a unique custom bike that is pretty much exactly what Russell told them to have ... which seems to be a recurring theme with Exile.

The bike has been given a long and low stance to make it look like it's doing 100mph standing still. A wise choice I think; after all, it will be spending a lot of time on static displays during major American bike events. Russell took his 'it must-be-painted black' mantra to the extreme, with extensive use of satin black powder coating throughout. He even had a revolutionary high-tech black coating

applied to the fork tubes, just so that he could black them out too! Only the stainless steel hardware that holds the motorcycle together was spared a coat of the dark stuff.

Of course, Russell gave his chosen painter, Buck Wild Design, enough artistic freedom to work in the satin gold racing stripe, and the repeating, but oh so subtle, Rockstar logo that graces the bike. The finished package ensured that Rockstar's new promotional tool had perfect lines and proportions, coupled with complete simplicity.

Russell employed all of the tricks that have become synonymous with Exile over the past decade to keep clutter to a sanitary bare minimum. For example, the bike features Exile's sprocket brake, to keep the rear wheel clean, and uses Exile's internal throttle, twist clutch kit and integrated brakes so that the bars are left clutter-free and understated. Pure class. It is touches like this that show Russell's relentless passion for motorcycles in general, and clinically clean choppers in particular.

Matching the bike's striking presence with performance was easy; Russell elected to use the incredible power that comes from a JIMS 131-inch Twin-Cam V-twin motor. This engine comes with Evolution-style lower mounts, and has been mated to a super smooth shifting JIMS 6-speed transmission. The 130bhp out-of-the-box lump boasts 135 ft/lbs of torque and comes with a full one-year warranty. As the trannie was built with large-capacity engines in mind, there are no worries there either. JIMS recently celebrated their fortieth anniversary of making performance-enhancing parts for Harley-Davidson motorcycles. It is rumoured that even The Factory themselves have called upon JIMS for technical assistance and R&D work.

Check out the word ROCKSTAR that has been machined into the heads, and the logos inserted in the ignition and clutch covers, and you will start to understand the level of thought, effort and work that this promo bike entailed. The 5-spoke billet wheels are a bit of a departure from Exile's usual Monster spoke offerings, so they were well outside Russell's comfort zone, however, he was more than happy with the way they looked once they had received the prescribed coating of black powder. Other features, like the three-inch open primary, the Monster shotgun pipes and the large round, dome ended oil-tank all help to give this bike the signature toughness that you have come to expect from Exile Cycles. Bill Wall Leather out-did themselves, producing the star-emblazoned saddle that crowned off the finished chopper. Rockstar are of course ecstatic with the finished result, just as Russell told them they would be. Oh, to have the ego of a Rockstar... **SK**

HARLEYS ON THE PAGE

Words: Steven Myatt

OUR ROUND-UP OF THE BEST H-D BOOKS

How many books have been written about the Harley-Davidson motorcycle over the years? No idea; I was hoping you would know. Whatever the total, it's certainly a lot, and we thought it would be an idea to have a good old look at what's around now. We set ourselves the task of selecting the six best books on the subject – which wasn't easy – and didn't include the huge number of books which are out of print but will still be available.

The best place to find the out-of-print volumes is the internet, needless to say, and Amazon and eBay are top of the list. Type Harley-Davidson into either and you get a whole lot of choice. There are also specialist sites which will find rare books for you, and these can be a great resource. The small town of Hay-on-Wye, on the Welsh-English border is one of the world's greatest centres of second-hand book shops, and they have an electronic catalogue of everything held by the town's dealers, which they will search for you – and for free (www.booksearch-at-hay.com).

We – which means me and Andy Hornsby of American-V – haven't included technical or one-model books, as that narrows the field too much. If you've got a Evo-engined bike then a book on restoring a Panhead is of limited use to you (though fascinating none the less ...).

First up is Everything You Need To Know – Harley Davidson Motorcycles, written by Bill Stermer. This is a really good first step sort of book, and don't be put off by the fact there's a photo of Lou Kimzey (one of the founders of Easyriders magazine) on the title page – looking like an older and less handsome version of myself (oh shut up at the back there), and sitting on a really ratty chop with utterly horrid forks.

Bill used to be Editorial Director of Rider magazine, and he's put together a very worthwhile 'starter' book. If you are a real Harley aficionado you might be a bit sniffy about it, but come on, everyone has to start somewhere. The book begins, logically enough, with a few pages on the company's history, then discusses choosing your first Harley (and dares to look at the alternatives – no, not Japanese

cruisers but Buells and other American V-twins). He moves on to look at customising, clothing and helmets – yes, all basic stuff, as I say. That's followed in due course by advice on basic performance and suspension upgrades, maintenance, and running a sidecar or a trike.

This book is very well illustrated with scores of colour photos, and towards the back you'll find a glossary of biker and Harley language. If you're just starting out on Harley ownership then this is a good first port of call.

Everything Harley-Davidson is by the same publisher and is in the same format; same number of pages, same size and similar design. There's a second line to the title though – A Century Of Memorabilia – and that explains what it's all about very concisely.

The book is a fascinating and beautifully presented compendium of Harley-Davidson's merchandising items down the years. Did you think that the company had only got into putting its name on stuff other than motorcycles in recent times? Think again!

Author Michael Dregni breaks it all down into seven categories, starting with the most obvious items; marketing material such as sales literature and little bits and pieces given to H-D dealers. It all goes way beyond that though.

A lot of the early sales literature is really charming. It promises the freedom of the open road, free of traffic, speed cops and inclement weather at all times. The guys riding the bikes (always guys riding, always with the girl safely – and smiling happily – on the back) are clean cut and eminently respectable. No hints of naughtiness anywhere. One gem is a binocular 3-D viewer which was a dealer give-away to promote the Topper scooter – with the slogan 'Set Your Sights On The Topper'. Find one of those on eBay, and in good condition, if you can.

There are all the usual sales incentives that any company offers; pens, rulers, ashtrays and other stuff for cluttering up your desk. But did you know that both Fender and Gibson offered Harley-Davidson branded guitars? Or made a promotional Harley penguin – yes, penguin – in the Seventies? Or a black powder pistol, in commemoration of the 75th anniversary of the V-twin engine? And as late as the 1990s there were Harley-Davidson cigarettes (in an appropriately funereal black packet); they wouldn't do that nowadays!

Branded clothing is a big part of the company's sales operation today, but as early as the Twenties they were selling caps, sweaters, and leather gaiters to protect the legs from hot oil.

There's a chapter on toy motorcycles, and while I don't know anyone who's life's mission is to collect all Harley memorabilia, I do know guys who go for these. They are, I must admit, really delightful and great fun. The earliest date from the Thirties, and over the years they've been made in a variety of materials and manufacturing techniques. Those early ones tend to be cast iron or pressed tin, and were obviously made in huge numbers and kept down to an economical price. I know that they are most valuable when they are in perfect, as-new condition and still have their original box, but I do prefer the examples that are worn – that have been loved and played with.

These are historical items in their own modest way. Each is of its time, and its design invariably reflects the period of its manufacture. In years to come archaeologists might well discover a Harley badge or cigarette lighter, and will be able to date it just as they'd date ancient pottery now.

Yes, it has a serious side too, in that it shows how a

company can fully exploit a successful brand, if you like. What other motorcycle manufacturer can lay claim to such an amazing spread of merchandising – but more importantly, it's great fun. Everything Harley-Davidson is a very attractively produced book and never anything less than a delight ... and I think I'll start collecting period Harley oil cans. And ... I wasn't going to mention this, but there is one crashing error, but I can't resist. Each chapter starts with a little blue drawing of a V-twin, which is fair enough, except that it very clearly isn't a Harley-Davidson. It's a Kawasaki VN1500. And I wouldn't like to have been the guy who dropped that clanger when the first copies arrived in from the printer.

The Harley-Davidson Reader is a very different beast indeed. This book is an anthology of thirty three pieces of writing about Harleys, sub-divided into eleven chapters with headings such as The Birth Of Bad, The Need For Speed and On The Road. They come from a huge range of writers, including well known motorcycling journalists such as Michael Dregni (again), Tim Remus and Allan Girdler, and more diverse names such as Craig Vetter, Sonny Barger and Hunter S Thompson (the latter being an excerpt from his classic book Hell's Angels: A Strange And Terrible Saga).

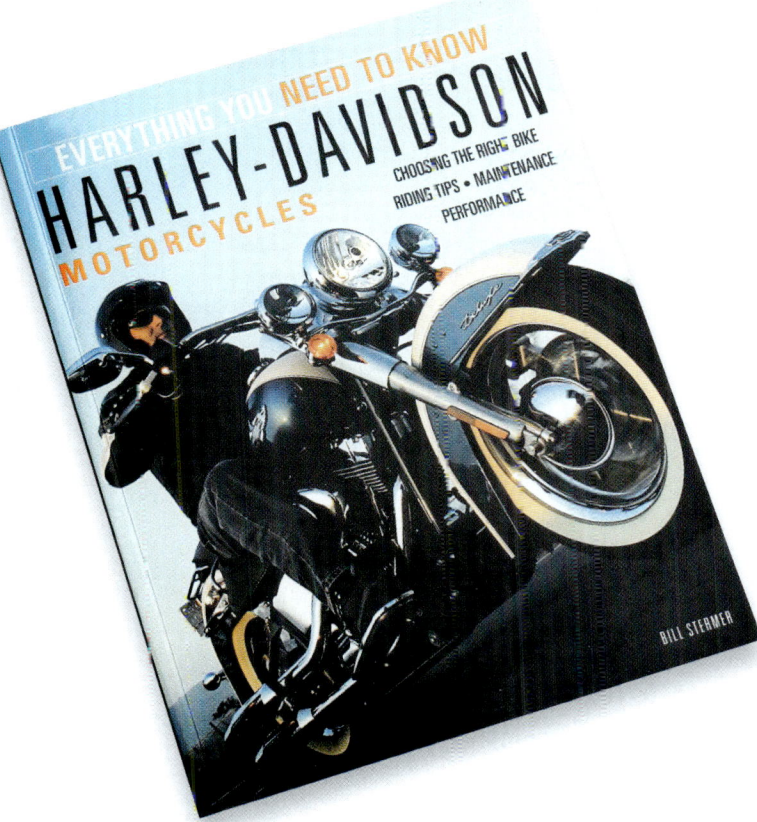

Knievel and I don't question it.' Evel Knievel, of course.

'From my mother I learned to write prompt thank-you notes for a variety of occasions; from Mrs King's ballroom dancing school I learned a proper curtsy and, believe it or not, what to do if presented with nine eating utensils at the same place setting, presumably at the home of the hosts to whom I had just curtsied. From motorcycles I learned practically everything else.' Melissa Holbrook Pierson.

'When my mood gets too hot and I find myself wandering beyond control I pull out my motor-bike and hurl it top-speed through these unfit roads for hour after hour. My nerves are jaded and gone near dead, so that nothing less than hours of voluntary danger will prick them into life.' T E Lawrence.

I said when I started that I wasn't going to include technical books in this review, but hey, life's full of these contradictions, isn't it? I'm going to go out and buy a Knucklehead just so that I can make good use of How To Restore Your Harley-Davidson by Bruce Palmer III. Having written half a dozen tomes in my time I know only too well how much work goes into writing a book, and this one just fills me with admiration. Is Bruce Palmer just one guy, who has worked on this

It has been very thoughtfully edited by Michael Dregni, and includes a foreword by Jean Davidson. It's peppered with quotations about riding motorcycles, and is illustrated with some excellent photographs – always appropriate to the piece in question. There are some great archive shots from the pioneer years, including a lot that I've never seen anywhere else, reproductions of both the covers of pulp biker novels and biker movie posters, and lots of period hand bills for races. It's a real cornucopia all things Harley, but with a lot of varied and really worthwhile reading central to its concept.

This is a book to really enjoy. I'd recommend that you set aside some time – and some beer, and perhaps a bit of something to eat – and settle in somewhere quiet, away from distractions. I'd say that it's a must for every fan of the Harley-Davidson motorcycle, but it goes beyond that; I can well imagine folk who have little interest in bikes really enjoying this book, too. A very classy production all round, and one that'll make you smile in places too. Highly recommended, and I can't leave it without sharing a few of the quotes I mentioned:

'I don't know why I did what I did. I did what I did because I'm Evel

of an issue out of that.

If you are restoring one of these models then this book will be worth it's weight in gold ... well, it's a hefty volume, weighing in at 4 lbs, and with the price of gold where it is just now you could buy a hell of a lot of perfectly restored Harleys and a museum to put them in. And just about anything else you had your heart set on. But you know what I mean ...

Military motorcycles are a minority fascination within the two wheel world, but no matter if you've never before given them a moment's thought – I defy you not to thoroughly enjoy Military Harley-Davidson by Pat Ware. There are enough facts and figures in this book to keep even the most passionate enthusiast happy, but it's the fuller story behind all that which had me entranced.

There's just so much to the subject, and from a standing start I found it truly absorbing. Pat's writing is very accessible- you don't need to be a military nut to follow the narrative, and although there are technical sections which you might skate over, there's plenty of other material to keep you reading. Military production played a big part in the story of Harley-Davidson, and I would argue that if you are a fan of their road bikes then you need to have a bit of perspective of this other side of the business to really appreciate the fuller picture.

Then there are the photos. And this is where the book scores yet again. Where did the author find all these incredible images? Indeed, who took all the shots in the first place (often in the least likely

for half a lifetime, or is it a pseudonym for a couple of dozen authors writing several hundred thousand words each?

As well as Knucklehead-engined bikes, the book covers Panheads, Big Twin side-valve machines, 45s and Servi-Cars. It's a breath-taking resource, covering absolutely every aspect of restoration you could think of. Got a problem with a broken petrol tank tab? Bruce will tell you how to fix it. Struggling with the manual advance dual-point timer? Refer to Bruce. Need to identify the right year of speedo, or find the right tonneau cover for a police-spec LE sidecar, or ream an errant clutch gear bushing? Check the index, turn the page, and this is where your problems will be solved.

It's illustrated with black and white photos throughout – which keeps the costs down; heaven knows what the price would be if it was full colour – and as well as the technical shots there's lots of interesting period photography too. Unsurprisingly, I've seen some of these photos before, but there are rarities too. The photo reproduction is a bit muddy at times, but it would be churlish of me to make too much

Motor Co. – Archive Collection is a glorious work, and a credit to its authors; photographer Randy Leffingwell and writer Darwin Holmstrom.

Published by renowned specialist, Motorbooks, this an authorised Harley publication, and the problem for me is to give you some idea of the book's enormous scope. Just about everything imaginably Harley is in between these beautifully-made covers. The only thing that it's not about is archive photography; there are other books for that, though there are a few period photos included; heading up each chapter. What we have here are photos of the company's collection of museum-quality machines.

The vast bulk of the photography was all shot in studio, which must have taken an age just to light – no production line work here – and the results are stunning. After the introduction (by Bill Davidson) and a few pages of background on the archive collection, we then embark on a chronological journey, starting with the 1903 Serial Number one. This machine isn't exactly the very first ever Harley; it has the numeral '1' stamped on a lot of its parts, but its internals show that it was a competition machine, and the frame may be a little later. It's as damn good as you're going to get though. It was completely restored in 1996-7 (and very, very carefully; you really wouldn't want to make a mistake with any of the components on this bike!) and is just about their greatest treasure.

We carry on through the single-cylinder bikes, and get into the V-twins with an unrestored 1912 Model 8-X-E, and after that we're on very familiar territory and we're away on a journey through the company's entire history. There are also a few period adverts, which are a delight – '27 Big Improvements. Let Your Dealer Point Them Out To You'. Okay, go on then.

Alongside the familiar there is also the extraordinary. There's 'Pop's Trolley', the 1930s ice yacht, powered by a propeller, which in turn was driven by a 1925 JDCB 74 ci engine. Assembled by Mead Gliders of Chicago, you could have had one, spruce and canvas body and all – for the huge sum of $149.50.

The early H-D bicycles are included, and though I'm no fan of two-wheeled machines without internal combustion engines, I must admit that the lightweight 1918 racer is a thing of great elegance, which still looks modern today.

Racers are included, of course, as are the Servi-Cars, military models (like the very rare XS three wheel-drive combo), the Japanese Harley (the Rikuo), and the hideous Model D-3 golf buggy. The Italian lightweights of the Sixties and Seventies are given equal billing, which I suppose is right and proper in the great scheme of things. The same is of course true of the AMF years.

There are custom bikes too (imagine that in a Honda or Kawasaki factory museum), starting with a very evocative Boozefighters-style WLA, and including replicas of both Billy's bike and the Captain America bike from Easy Rider (and for me it's always been Billy's bike that I'd want to ride away on). Plus ... well, hey, there's Elvis on his K-Model; there's Joe Petrali's streamliner; the gorgeous KRTT road racer, and that 2003 Ultra Classic Electra Glide combo with 1,000 staff signatures on it. Whatever your favourite model of Harley – for my money, since you ask, a '36 EL Knucklehead, a mid-Fifties FLF Pan, a bare naked XR-750, a black-as-night XLCR, or, yes, Billy's bike – you'll find it here and you'll be able to see every detail. A splendid book, and one which demonstrates why reading books on-line will never kill off print and paper. **SM**

circumstances)? I have a great passion for old photos, and this book made me a very happy man. I wanted to know the stories behind each and every one of them. Look, there we see two Japanese soldiers in a Harley combo (yep, with right-hand sidecar) in about 1920. Here we see a beautifully framed and composed shot of a group of American soldiers (and a scruffy little dog) sitting round a WLA in the courtyard of a ruined French farmhouse. Over the page there's a portrait of an immaculately turned-out member of the Chicago police department (a small but acceptable side-line) with his single-cylinder Harley in 1908. I can – and did – spend hours just looking at the photos, imagining the story behind the scene frozen in time. (Talking of frozen, there's a shot of a Model J-mounted soldier waiting for a camera to be unloaded from a World War One bi-plane, as it sits with its propeller still turning in inches of snow).

It's to the publisher's credit that the book is printed on very good quality paper, and the photo reproduction is excellent. Some of the early prints must have originated on large glass plates; the quality of the detail is stunning. Gosh, it just makes me want to find a WLA (and I know someone who's got one ... see elsewhere in this publication) so that I can start shooting at the enemy with a Thompson gun.

Now, we come to the big one – or should that be THE BIG ONE? I thought that How To Restore Your Harley-Davidson was a hefty volume, but this is just madness. It's taken two strong men and an industrial hoist just to get it on to my desk. The Harley-Davidson

TRY THIS AT HOME

The road beckons but the accountant says no?
Worried about your carbon footprint?
There has never been a better time to go nowhere.
Live vicariously through the tales of Mr Mutch. Marvel at his exploits riding hard
tail chops off road through the Negev desert. Salivate as he troughs on buffalo
burger in Kansas city and lobster in St Tropez.
Wince as he shudders a 1600cc Harley-Davidson through a Mauritanian
minefield. Laugh cruelly as he runs out of fuel in the West Bank.
No records broken, just self indulgent and seriously inept motorcycle travel.

Plus Motorcycles Forever - a pictorial history of biker culture and the fight for
freedom on wheels from the President of The Motorcycle Action Group and
Harley rider since 1981.

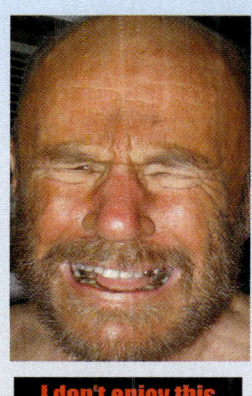

I don't enjoy this
you know

Just out!

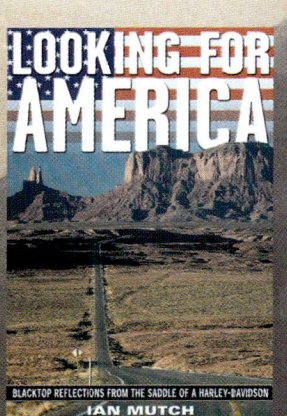

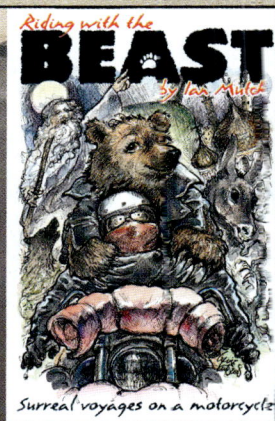

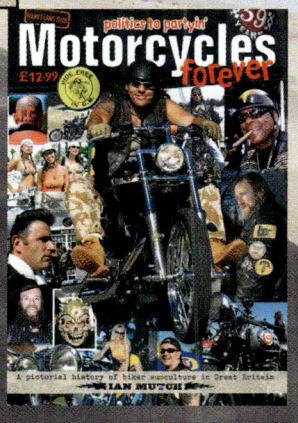

All five for £35 inc P&P

"YOU'RE JUST A HOP-HEAD WITH A BIG OL' BIKE"

THE GREATEST HARLEY MOVIE EVER MADE – AND NO, IT'S NOT EASY RIDER

Put the word 'movie' and the name 'Harley-Davidson' together in the same sentence and the odds are heavily in favour of the words 'Easy Rider' also ending up in there too. Easy Rider is a hugely important film for very many reasons, and it gave a huge boost to the biker culture. But is it the best Harley movie ever made? Were Harleys absolutely crucial to the plot of the film? Really?

Granted, Fonda and Hopper would have struggled to establish the contemporary counter culture if they were ambling down to New Orleans in a Greyhound bus; you can only watch the moon rising over an open field for so long. But what if they had been in a Dodge Challenger or a '55 Chevy street racer (as in Vanishing Point and Two Lane Blacktop, respectively)? Would they have had the same adventures – good, bad and tragic – along the way? It's possible, you know; it really is. It's a strange contention to make, but Easy Rider could have been just as effective and successful if there wasn't a Harley to be seen in a single frame. Now there's a thought.

You can't say that of The Loveless though. You could no more have made The Loveless without bikes than you could make omelettes without eggs, or beer without hops. And whereas Easy Rider is a 'buddy' movie, The Loveless is a gang movie. A gang in the loosest sense, as in a group of similar-minded people with a common aim and intent, but a gang none the less. It's an 'us against the world' film just as much as in Easy Rider, but the greasers in The Loveless have no interest in changing society, much as they might despise it (and oh boy, they do!). Billy and Wyatt want to turn the whole world on. Vance and Davis don't give a flying kick start return spring for changing society, for better or worse. And isn't it Scientologists and Hare Krishna devotees who proselytise – handing out improving leaflets and ▸

Words: Steven Myatt
Illustration: Gareth Williams

looking for converts on door-steps – rather than Harley riders? Yes, it is.

Above all, Easy Rider is a film about failing to survive, against the odds. The Loveless is quite the opposite. You don't really expect any one of the Harley riders to make it through to the end credits, but they do. They get to ride away.

No, much as I love it, much as it has had a huge impact on my life, Easy Rider is a great biker movie, but not the ultimate Harley movie. But hang on, talking of the greatest biker movies, we do have to go back a few years, of course, and think about The Wild One.

It wasn't the first biker movie but it was the first which was truly influential, and which showed the world the emerging outlaw biker culture – however credible it does or does not look in the film.

The real hero of The Wild One wasn't, of course, the buttoned-up and basically decent character played by Marlon Brando. You get the feeling that he was going through a bit of a bad patch – as if he'd been fired from his job and then his dog had died – and in a few months he would snap out of it, buy a shirt with a button-down collar and get a job to go with it, put a down-payment on a little place in the suburbs and start going to church on Sundays.

Lee Marvin's character, Chino, is a completely different kettle of hoodlum. He's a real outsider – bordering on being a sociopath – and you'd only see him in a button-down shirt if a mortician with a bizarre sense of humour put one on his corpse. Chino is a volcano waiting to erupt; utterly unpredictable and terminally volatile. He represented both the emerging Beat culture and the biker lifestyle that was growing up in the States in the Fifties. He's a Rabelaisian freewheeler; a genuine, no-holds-barred bohemian.

He's the one that's roaring drunk, not Johnny. He's the one that fights dirty, not Johnny. Not for him smart black leather. Black leather is worn to protect the skin and flesh in an accident; Chino isn't interested

in that – he'd be so drunk that he'd just bounce when he fell off.

But of course it's Chino who rides a Harley in the film, not Johnny. Johnny rides a then-new and completely stock Triumph. It would have been a very sensible choice in 1953; fast, reliable and manoeuvrable – but hardly an outlaw bike. An advertising executive who ran a Buick during the week might have a Triumph for running around on at the weekends. Chico, on the other hand, rides a quintessential early custom bike – a cut-down, probably ex-military Harley with no front mudguard and, in fact, nothing on it at all that wasn't essential to its basic purpose of going and stopping.

There's a lot of Chico to be seen in Vance, Davis, La Ville, Hurley and Ricky – the bike gang of The Loveless. Well, when I say 'bike gang' that's not quite right. They're a motley group of guys – hardly a bike gang and certainly without a club name or identity – who just happen to have a few things in common. They're simply into bikes – and the bikes are Harleys – and everything that goes with them at that far-off-on-the-horizon end of the spectrum.

That's one thing, but they're also complete social misfits too. Like Chico, these guys wouldn't know how to compromise if their life depended on it, and in fact one day it might well do. What matters is the moment; the speed, the beer and the good times – though throughout the movie they are very pointedly not having much of a good time at all. They're utter nihilists; the telling shot is the blade going into the upholstery of the truck stop booth – no reason to do that, but then, no reason not to either. Similarly, when the waitress struts through her striptease at the roadhouse she's met with soul-destroying disdain.

All the characters in the film are utterly, thoroughly and completely unpleasant – to say the least. They have no redeeming factors, and apart from the young waitress, widowed five years ago and dreaming of getting away (something you know she will never do) – there's not an ounce of humanity between them.

The five Harley riders – finger-clickin' members of the leather-clad far end of the Beat generation; all Howl and no poetry – loathe, distrust and despise each other, and have none of the sense of loyalty which holds a group together. They need each other and are reassured by the presence of the others, but they certainly don't like each other. There's also a girl in tow; Sportster Debbie, all bottle-blonde hair, tight slacks and high heels. Sexy as you like if you don't mind unfortunate diseases. She's Davis's girlfriend in theory, but anyone's in reality, and doesn't particularly mind who knows it. Where d'you find a really naughty girl like that when you need one?

In a way it's a post-punk film. There's nothing of the idealism you see in Easy Rider (the idealism which, though glorious, in fact comes to nothing). There are no common bonds other than rootlessness and nihilism. The five bikers are treading water before their next jail term, or until their Harleys simply run out of road for the last time. For now they're a triumph of oily hair preparations, and not a crash helmet in sight – would have messed up the hairstyle more than the wind did.

We're not told when the film is set, but the bikes are all Fifties models and the newest car in the film is Tarver's '59 Chevrolet Impala, though it certainly doesn't look brand new (the way he drives it does it no favours). Talena's Corvette could be a '58, '59 or '60 model, and it was some time ago – when her mother shot herself – that she came by it. The Thunderbird we see near the start is a '57. There are flashes of dialogue on car radios discussing the Cold War. So, minor detective work tells us that it could be 1959 or 1960.

All the characters in the film are utterly, thoroughly and completely unpleasant – to say the least

We are also not told where it's set, but it's certainly the Deep South; indeed there is a condiment on a shelf in the kitchen named just that. The accents – always so perfect – tell us the same thing. There's a passing reference to Highway 17, of which there are several in the USA, of course – however there is a Highway 17 in central, deepest Alabama, and my money's on that. It's certainly a possible route from Chicago to Florida (the bikers are off to Daytona to catch the races). That puts them south of Birmingham, next stop Montgomery (which is the surname of one of the writers and directors ...). As for the 'when', well the main racing season for motorbikes at Daytona is March, so we can assume it's set in the spring.

The film's action takes place over a single day and evening, and within a very small horizon. The bikers arrive at a diner on the edge of a small rural town – well, at least we're told that there's a town but we only ever see the diner, an edge-of-town garage, a run-down black-run moonshine outfit, a motel, and a roadhouse. The common ▶

Finger-clickin' members of the leather-clad far end of the Beat generation; all Howl and no poetry

denominator is claustrophobia and boredom. All the lives are lived within a tiny area and there is absolutely nothing to do – apart from drink coffee in the daytime and beer at night, watch NASCAR on TV and read girlie magazines. Nothing happens. Ever. The talk of Daytona hints at wide open vista and sunshine, but what we see is exactly the opposite. It's a world of rusty pickup trucks, cheap cigarettes and 10-cent Cokes, in a landscape hemmed in on all side by dense woodland.

The film starts with the voice of Robert Gordon; setting the scene as he sings, 'I was born over-heated under a blue-black sky' to a splendid rockabilly beat. Then we see Vance, moody in his shades, zipping up his leather jacket in the cold dawn light, and slowly firing up his Panhead. It fires second kick. In a moment he'll tell us that he's just out

of jail, and that he's going to hell in a bread-basket, but for now – as he rides off down the deserted blacktop – his mono-tone voiceover announces; 'Man, I was what you call ragged. I mean, way beyond torn up. I wasn't going to be no man's friend today'. And you get the distinct impression that makes today the same as yesterday, and tomorrow will be much the same too.

Vance plays white knight to a damsel in distress, changing the wheel on her T-Bird. Well, not a very white knight – more dark grey; he does the job but takes all her money and grabs a very forceful kiss. And as for a damsel in distress, it turns out she's a hooker. Quite a well paid one, I'd guess; a Ford Thunderbird was a $3,500+ car in 1957 (an average working man's wage was around $4,500).

Vance stops at a roadside diner – The Liberty Truck Center – to wait for the other gang members, and a bad primary drive chain means that they have to find a garage to carry out repairs. The locals – all but one of the waitresses, that is, younger and still pretty – treat them with fear and disdain. The exception is called Augusta; she treats them with fear, disdain ... and a degree of fascination. She tries to make conversation with Vance but is quickly rebuffed. Perhaps she's strangely drawn to men in greasy undergarments.

As they're fixing the Harley, the interestingly-named Talena, who turns out to be a daddy's girl in more ways than one, turns up in a gorgeous open-top Corvette. Vance isn't a biker of the 'two wheels good, four wheels bad' mindset, and he hustles her for a ride in the

BIKER MOVIES: HOW THEY RATE

CC And Company (1970)
Ann-Margaret rocks (as ever) ★★★☆☆

Crazy Baby (1968)
Second rate British Mods & Rockers ★★☆☆☆

Born To Ride (1991)
1930s bikers fight Nazis ★☆☆☆☆

The Leather Boys (1964)
A British Rocker classic ★★★★☆

The Angry Breed (1969)
Vietnam veteran biker is bonkers ★★☆☆☆

Black & Chrome (2000)
Beyond seriously strange ★★★☆☆

Harley Davidson And The Marlboro Man (1991)
Two American legends! ★★☆☆☆

Motorcycle Gang (1994)
Truly, truly awful ★☆☆☆☆

Cycle Savages (1969)
With a title like that must be good ★★★☆☆

Angel Unchained (1970)
Bruce Dern, how could you? ★★☆☆☆

The Great Escape (1969)
Not a biker movie but there's *that* jump ★★★☆☆

Girls From Thunder Strip (1966)
Groovy hippy chicks on bikes ★★☆☆☆

The Motorcycle Diaries (2004)
For commie Che Guevara fans only ★★☆☆☆

The World's Fastest Indian (2005)
True story of Burt Monro. Terrific ★★★★★

Savages From Hell (1968)
Fun after a few beers too many ★★☆☆☆

Motorcycle Gang (1957)
Unbelievably cheesy but good fun ★★☆☆☆

Teenage Devil Dolls (1955)
Low budget tale of reefer abuse. Mmm ★★★☆☆

Hell's Angels '69 (1969)
Great for a biker flick ★★★☆☆

Chrome & Black Leather (1971)
Marvin Gaye! Yes, honestly. Wow ★★★☆☆

Run Angel Run (1969)
... From the critics, at least ★☆☆☆☆

Ivy League Killers (1962)
Delinquent preppies fight bikers ★☆☆☆☆

It's a world of rusty pickup trucks, cheap cigarettes and 10-cent Cokes

car that daddy has bought her – bought her for reasons which become clear later.

She reveals that her mother has committed suicide, which is again laying down something of a marker, and also assures Vance that 'I just know I could take you to heaven'. Coming from the perfectly-formed mouth of a girl who appears to be little more than fourteen or fifteen, it's far, far sexier than it ought to be. So off they go to book into a motel to do the obvious thing, having bought some hooch from the 'darkies'.

Then Daddy – Tarver – turns up, and in a fit of what we can certainly assume is jealousy, peppers the 'Vette with a couple of blasts from a shotgun. He grabs the naked Talena as Vance hides his modesty, and she rather heavy-handedly tells him 'He ain't done nothin' t'me that you ain't done a hundred times before' and we get the picture.

Tarver is gloriously played by the late J Don Ferguson, who actually ▶

HARLEY GIRLS IN THE MOVIES

Marin Kanter, who played the gorgeous young jail-bait in The Loveless was actually 22 when she acted in that role (you'd have sworn she was 15 at the most, wouldn't you?). Born in Cincinnati, she had appeared in a movie called Ladies And Gentlemen: The Fabulous Stains. In the film she's one of three girls (one other being Laura Dern) who start a band. There's a heavy British contingent in there too, including the then-young and slender Ray Winstone, plus Steve Jones and Paul Cook of the Sex Pistols and Paul Simonon of The Clash.

Beyond that, her film credits don't seem to have been extensive, but in 1991 she starred in the comedy Too Much Sun, which was directed by Robert Downey Snr and starred Downey and ex-Python Eric Idle. Marin plays a character named Tiny Nun, which sounds interesting but I didn't want to displace my mental image of her lying naked on the motel bed in The Loveless so I decided not to investigate further.

Tina L'Hotsky played the gloriously filthy Sportster Debbie in The Loveless. She had been a fixture of the chic New York scene in the late Sixties and Seventies, and described herself as The Queen of The Mud Club (the epicentre of the East River avant garde world). Born in Cleveland, Ohio in 1952, one of twelve siblings, she had shortened her name from Christine Lhotsky. She died of breast cancer in August 2008, having lived in Pasadena in California for twenty years. She described herself as an artist, writer and actress, though the only other film she seems to have been in was the short Stiletto in 1981.

Easy Rider is, if you think about it, very much a male film. The first woman we see is the rancher's Mexican wife, and then there are the two girls in the hippie commune. Both those actresses had worthwhile careers. They were played by Liana Anders and Sabrina Scharf. Luana

died in California (like Tina L'Hotsky, of breast cancer) in 1996 at the age of 58. She had a very distinguished career, appearing in 77 movies and TV shows. She encouraged the young Jack Nicholson to act, was in the glorious horror flick The Pit And The Pendulum with Vincent Price, and also Shampoo with Warren Beatty. She acted in many well-known TV series such as Little House on the Prairie, Bonanza, Ironside, Dragnet 1967, The Outer Limits and Hawaii Five-O.

Sabrina had also been in Hawaii Five-O and went on to appear in the Man From UNCLE and some thirty films. She was also in the great biker B-movie Hell's Angels On Wheels (which starred the very young, pre-Easy Rider Jack Nicolson as Poet), which was a nice contrast with her one-off role as a Native American tribeswoman in an episode of Star Trek. She started her career as a Bunny Girl at the New York City Playboy Club and ended it in politics – becoming a state senator for California.

Another Easy Rider actress who had a fascinating career was Carmen Phillips who played one of the mime artists. Born in 1937 she started her working life as a showgirl, but had been an ever-busy actress since appearing in an Alfred Hitchcock TV show in 1958. In later life she was a committed animal rights activist. She died of lung cancer in September 2002 and the memorials were lead by her friend Diane Ladd.

And did you ever wonder what became of Mary Murphy, who played Kathie Bleeker, the goodie-goodie daughter of the town sheriff in The Wild One, who rather fell for bad boy Johnny? Born in Washington DC in 1931, she starred in about 70 movies between 1951 and the mid-Seventies. Things then went quiet for her and in the Eighties (after an appearance in a Steve McQueen film) she retired. To the best of my knowledge she's still with us.

came from Savannah in Georgia, so was a real Southerner – and died there in October 2008, aged 74. He's a study in red-neck rage, whether powering his Chevy across the dirt, cheating the hard-pressed waitress in the diner or threatening others into submission. He's never on screen without the veins in his neck bulging in fury. Literally a

---

You can almost hear Bigelow or Montgomery stopping the filming and telling Dafoe that he's still moving too fast

---

redneck, then. Looks like a coronary waiting to happen.

He drags his daughter off but crashes his Impala, coming off the road and hitting a tree as he tries to avoid the other bikers. He's unhurt but his daughter suffers facial injuries, to go with the facial scar that he inflicted on her some time ago. She's just one of life's victims, I guess.

Darkness falls and we shift to the roadhouse lounge, and if anything the walls come in even closer as the sense of inevitable, claustrophobic doom intensifies. The young waitress has still got half an eye on Vance but he couldn't care less. She asks Vance if he likes their town and he replies, talking to a woman we know was widowed a few years ago, 'I think your husband had the right idea'. Not a gentlemanly response. ▶

The Wild One (1954)
Whaddyamean you never heard of it? ★★★★★

Satan's Sadists (1969)
Mo'sickle mayhem in the Mojave desert ★★☆☆☆

Hell's Bloody Devils (1970)
Bikers, the Mafia, FBI, Nazis ... ★☆☆☆☆

The Losers (1970)
Bikers go to fight in Vietnam ★☆☆☆☆

Harley (1990)
Trust me on this; avoid at all costs ★☆☆☆☆

Dragstrip Riot (1958)
Good boy gets bike and goes bad ★★★☆☆

Electra-Glide In Blue (1973)
A real Seventies classic ★★★★☆

Mad Max (1979)
Inspired the matt black survival bike cult ★★★★☆

The Mini Skirt Mob (1968)
Talk about greased nipples! ★★☆☆☆

Werewolves On Wheels (1971)
Great if watched while drunk ★★★☆☆

Knightriders (1981)
CBX-riders jousting at a pageant (daft) ★☆☆☆☆

Crazy Baby (1968)
Strange period piece, best avoided ★☆☆☆☆

The Long Ride (1998)
Largely uninspiring ★★☆☆☆

Death Riders (1994)
Bikers go treasure hunting ★★☆☆☆

Viva Knievel! (1977)
Stars Evel himself – and Gene Kelly ★★☆☆☆

Easy Rider (1969)
What is there to say? A true classic ★★★★★

Hell's Angels On Wheels (1967)
The very best of the '60s biker genre ★★★★☆

Evel Knievel (1971)
George Hamilton is just too smooth ★★★☆☆

She Devils On Wheels (1968)
Butch biker babes raise hell ★★★☆☆

The Stranger (1995)
A sort of martial arts biker movie ★★☆☆☆

Motorcycle Squad (1937)
Great for its age; the first bike movie? ★★★☆☆

Motor Psycho (1965)
Lovely low-rent Russ Meyer period piece ★★☆☆☆

She dances a moody but – it must be said, rather bored and uninspiring (you really can't smoke and strip at the same time) – burlesque striptease to a splendid rockabilly backtrack, only to be roundly insulted for her troubles. A '55 Chevy hot rod blows its motor on the highway, for no obvious reason other than to form a punctuation mark, and tell you that the real action isn't far away.

The film ends with ... well, in case you haven't seen it, I won't tell you. There's a great late-night drunken scene in the roadhouse – including

A '55 Chevy hot rod blows its motor on the highway, for no obvious reason other than to form a punctuation mark

accusations that the bikers are, horror of horrors, communists; which is a likely as them being Carmelite nuns in disguise – and everything goes to hell, as Vance predicted right at the outset.

Tarver has been talking his dim-witted brother into an Easy Rider shotgun-fest out on the highway, but events overtake him.

Everything has moved so slowly until this point, but now it erupts in all directions. Such a shame that Talena didn't just jump on the back of Vance's bike and head off to Florida with him and the gang. It would have been too tidy an ending though, and he's not the sort of guy who likes to be encumbered by such a drag as a pillion passenger.

The Loveless was made in 1982, co-written and co-directed by Kathryn Bigelow and Monty Montgomery. It was the first film project for both of them, which only makes it more of an achievement. The film wasn't universally well received when it opened. One reviewer – Janet Maslin – got really stuck in, calling it 'a pathetic homage to the 1950s', and adding 'Vance spends a lot of time zipping and unzipping his jacket expressively and presumably embodies the ultimate in tough chic. The closest Vance comes to expressing any emotion is when another character commits the hippest act he can imagine. It's suicide, and Vance, while a little bit sorry, is mostly impressed.'

Another reviewer described the script of The Loveless as being 'almost entirely without depth or interest', but did concede that 'Bigelow and Montgomery make the most of virtually every shot – the compositions and use of colour are frequently striking', and 'Dafoe is every bit as cool as the movie requires'. There's also praise for the soundtrack, and quite rightly too.

That soundtrack is the work of Robert Gordon, who also plays Davis in the film. He sorted all the music and also wrote and sang on some of the songs. Born in Bethesda, Maryland in 1947, Gordon was singing with a group called The Confidentials by 1964. The mid-Seventies saw him fronting New York punk-era band The Tuff Darts as part of the

Then Came Bronson (1969)
The young Martin Sheen goes riding
★★★☆☆

On Any Sunday (1971)
Hillclimbing, financed by Steve McQueen
★★★★☆

Psychomania (1974)
The devil-worshipping biking undead
★★☆☆☆

Under Hot Leather (1971)
Beware, contains nuns!
★★★☆☆

Renegade (1993)
Ex-cop becomes two-wheeled avenger
★★☆☆☆

Road Kill (1999)
Actually quite a bit of a laugh
★★★☆☆

Roadside Prophets (1992)
Timothy Leary, Arlo Guthrie, Beastie Boys!
★★★☆☆

The Loveless (1982)
Stylish, sexy, great bikes
★★★★★

Quadrophenia (1979)
Great British Mod-fest
★★★★★

Run Angel Run (1969)
Another of the great biker flicks
★★★☆☆

Leather And Iron (2002)
Has a character called Chopper. Awful
★☆☆☆☆

Rebel Rousers (1970)
Jack Nicholson again!
★★☆☆☆

Little Fauss & Big Halsy (1970)
Great music on biker buddy story
★★★☆☆

The Wild Angels (1966)
Peter Fonda + Nancy Sinatra = Classy
★★★★☆

Running Cool (1993)
Bone and Bear ride to Sturgis
★★☆☆☆

The Glory Stompers (1967)
Dennis Hopper pre-Easy Rider
★★☆☆☆

Girl On A Motorcycle (1968)
Boring but fuelled so many sexual fantasies
★★★★☆

Angels Hard As They Come (1971)
Meant to be satire, apparently
★☆☆☆☆

Angels Die Hard (1970)
Bikers save lives after a mining disaster
★☆☆☆☆

The Indian (2007)
Didn't get the distribution it deserved
★★★☆☆

CBGB scene along with The Ramones and Blondie. He was never a punk though; his inspirations were soul and classic Fifties rock 'n roll. He was introduced to guitarist Link Wray and went back to his roots, becoming a flag-waver for rockabilly. Their 1978 album Fresh Fish Special was perfect rock 'n roll, and the same year Bruce Springsteen wrote the song Fire for him, though his version of that was rather eclipsed by that of The Pointer Sisters. For many years he has worked with the British guitarist Chris Spedding (author of the deeply annoying 1975 single Motorbikin', and – though he's played guitar with everyone from Paul McCartney to Kate Melua – most often seen with Roxy Music these days) who is also a devotee of Fifties rock 'n roll.

Casting Robert as Davis in The Loveless was an act of utter genius. Davis is sneering, edgy, unpredictable and lascivious. Border-line psychotic, in fact. You'd swear that he's pepped up to his deep brown eyeballs every waking moment. The script that Bigelow and Montgomery gave him is perfect, and he delivers it utterly convincingly. Having stopped to ask directions, he's asked where he's come from; sneering gloriously he replies; 'It doesn't matter which way I'm coming from. It's where I'm going to.' And in the diner he eyes the young waitress's posterior and asks, 'Hey, you on the menu?' Robert was 35 when he the film was shot but the feel of the character he plays succeeds in being ten years younger.

Willem Dafoe is cool as ice as the movie's hero (or anti-hero, I guess). He's stylish, hip and deeply threatening every moment he's on screen. It's hard to think of anyone who could have carried that part more effectively, and he oozes star quality. He also carries the directors' pace ▶

Please note that some movies have had alternative titles

very well. Action is easy; inaction is much harder. You can almost hear Bigelow or Montgomery stopping the filming and telling Dafoe that he's still moving too fast, and that he needs to count three beats between each word. It's very daring – silence is always daring – and his amazing presence on screen ensures success.

As well as being taciturn and brooding, if you look carefully you'll see that he always has a real biker's greasy fingers and broken fingernails, which is a nice touch. He exudes star quality, with his wicked, sexy smile, and his aura of meanness. He gets to speak some great lines too. Oh yes, and he gets to be naked in bed with Marin Kanter, lucky devil.

Dafoe went on to see real movie stardom, of course – including Spiderman, The English Patient, Mississippi Burning, American Psycho, Platoon and dozens of other high-profile and very well received movies. He has a reputation for being a non-Hollywood, independent-minded actor, and he has always worked in low-earning, art house movies and theatres in tandem with his commercial successes. Born in 1955, he was 27 when The Loveless came out.

None of the other actors in The Loveless went on to great things, and almost all seem to have dropped out of the acting scene completely. Of the two writers and directors, Kathryn Bigelow has had the more distinguished career since the film was made.

Strikingly tall and beautiful, she was known as an artist, and has gone on to have a fascinating career as a director. She is best known for the modern-day vampire movie Near Dark, Blue Steel with Jamie Lee Curtis, and Point Break with a debut performance from Keanu Reeves. Her 1995 movie Strange Days was well received by the critics but was not a commercial success. That flop seemed to have a disproportionately harsh impact on her career. Since then she has directed for television, made a music video with New Order and been a judge at innumerable film festivals.

In 2000 she directed both *The Weight of Water* and *K-19: The Widowmaker* about a doomed Russian nuclear submarine during the Cold War. In 1989 she married film director James Cameron – most famously director of Titanic – but the marriage only lasted two years. They have collaborated on a number of projects since. Her latest film is The Hurt Locker, which is set in Iraq and was released in October 2008.

Monty Montgomery – not to be confused with guitarist Monte Montgomery – has made films with figures as diverse as David Lynch and Michael Jackson, and has been responsible for a number of TV commercials, as well as working as a film and television producer. He also acted in the 2001 film Mulholland Drive. His real name is Lafayette Montgomery.

Two last points; I've seen reference to The Loveless with the alternative title 'Breakdown'. I don't know if it was released anywhere with that name – but I do hope not. Unless it referred to the bike breaking down with the bad primary chain (I'm joking), then it must refer to Talena, and that would be very wrong because it would shift the emphasis on to her and away from the Harley riders.

Finally, one other contributor to this publication (mentioning no names but you know who you are, Bob) told me, when I said that I was going to be writing about The Loveless, that it was a gay film. Is it? I've always found it a very sexy movie indeed – be it the rich red of Talena's Corvette or the perfect curve of her back-side – but I can see why anyone might think that it's a gay flick. There's lots of rippling male muscles, hot and sweaty bare chests, creaking black leather and bulging crotches ... and on balance, I don't really care. This is the greatest Harley movie ever made, and whether you're gay, straight or a dead hamster I recommend it to you too. And having said that, I'm going to kick over my stripped down Hydra-Glide and rumble off into the twilight – the smell of cordite and a rockabilly beat still hanging in the cool evening air. **SK**

HARLEY'S EARLY RIVALS

AND THE HEROES WHO BUILT AND RODE THEM

Harley-Davidson are – **quite needless to say** – the virtually undisputed kings of motorcycle manufacturing in the USA, but it wasn't always so. Over the hundred-and-something years that motorbikes have been made, there have been around 300 companies making motorcycles commercially across the country and offering those machines to the general public. There are some amazing stories behind many of them. Stories of ingenuity and invention, and behind them all, some truly exceptional men – to whom we all owe a great debt. In our enthusiasm for Harleys we mustn't close our eyes to these remarkable men: here's a look at just a few of them.

GLENN CURTISS

In a round-up of early two-wheel heroes there's no way that anyone could ever by-pass Glenn H Curtiss. Curtiss was born in 1878 in Hammondsport, New York, and had a very limited education. Not that the fact ever held him back. His first job was as a bicycle messenger for Western Union, and this lead him first to bicycle races, and then on to motorcycle racing just as soon as the internal combustion engine was dropped into a push bike frame. By the end of the Nineteenth century he had his own bicycle shop.

As early as 1902 a machine he had built achieved the fastest time at the New York Motorcycle Club road races. A year later he won the club's hill climb, which had attracted riders from all over America, and by 1904 he was competing in the Ormond Beach speed trials in Florida. His best time for a ten mile run was 67.4 mph, which wasn't beaten until 1908 – quite remarkable given how quickly motorcycle technology was evolving.

In 1904 Curtiss invented the handlebar throttle control – and you've been all these years wondering who we had to thank for that, eh? In the same year he saw his motorcycle engine installed at the power plant in a hydrogen-filled dirigible.

Not one to sit back and dust his laurels, Curtiss starting working on a new machine. He had been developing a V8 engine for use in an aircraft, but what could be better than dropping it into a bike frame? It was a curious looking machine, and was all of seven feet long. The front forks were steered with rods which pivoted from halfway along the very lengthy bars. It had shaft final drive and an open differential.

He returned to Ormond Beach with it in 1907, and had the bike towed until it hit 40 mph, before being setting loose under its own

Words: Steven Myatt
Illustration: Louise Limb

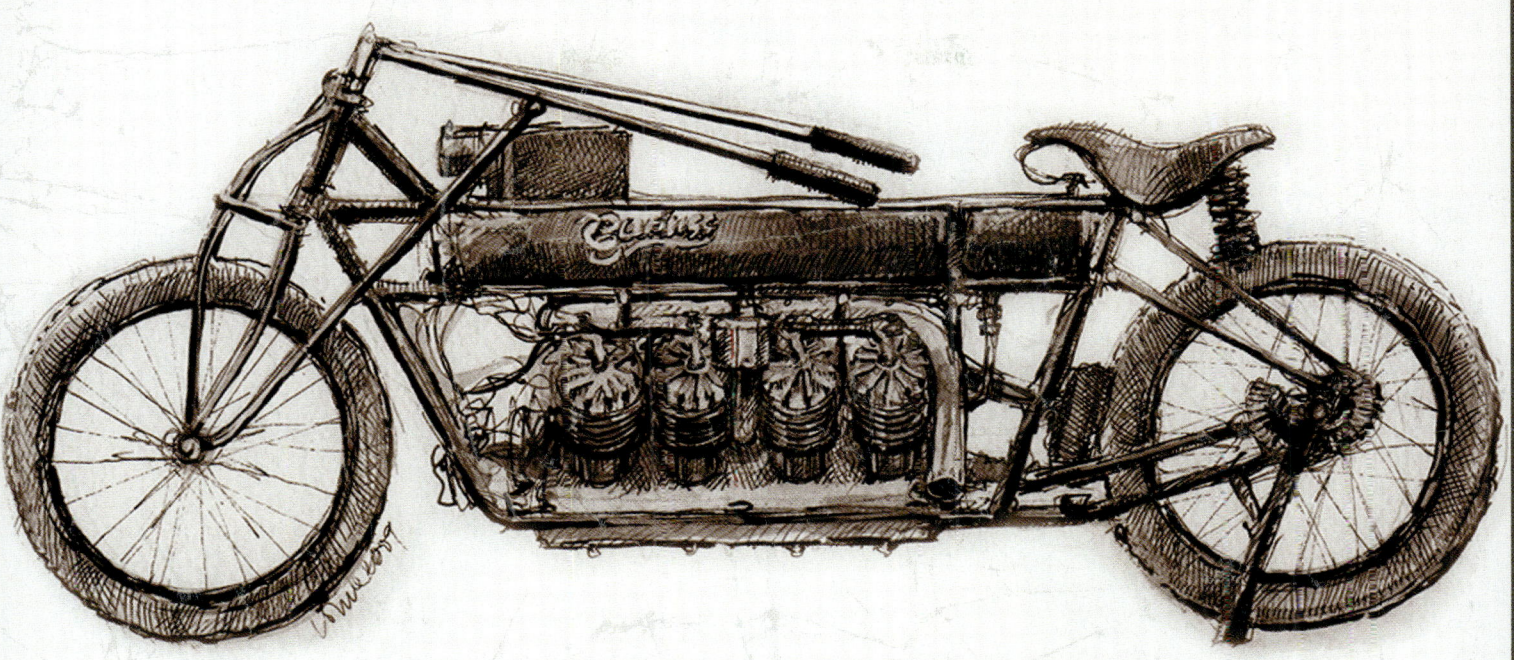

power. It hit a truly astonishing 136.3 mph – we're talking about 1907, remember? – but couldn't complete a second run as the final drive failed. This meant that Curtiss didn't officially have a record time, though it was another 23 years before anyone hit that speed on two wheels again. Unofficially he had travelled faster than any other human being had ever done before. Can you imagine what that must have felt like back then? What a hero.

By that date he was part of the very distinguished Aerial Experimental Association which was intent on manned flight (their number included Alexander Graham Bell), and it's known that he visited the Wright brothers in 1906 and discussed aviation technology. In 1909 he became America's first licensed manufacturer of aircraft, and that year he also established the first licensed flying school.

He made his first motorcycle in 1902, just two years after he had started making bicycles. He called his early bikes Hercules (as the push bikes had been), and they quickly evolved. By 1908 they were powered by a 2.5 horsepower single with a forward-mounted carb. The exhaust had a silencer cut-out lever for more speed (and greater noise!).

After a legal dispute with a Californian-based company which was also using the name Hercules, Curtiss affixed his own surname to the bikes, and in 1903 introduced a V-twin. This lovely-looking bike was the first V-twin motorcycle offered to the American public, and was powered by a 1,000 cc motor and weighed just 160 lbs. It cost $275, which wasn't cheap by the standards of the day, but it was good for around 60 mph. It had long, pull-back handlebars and belt-driven final drive.

When the First World War loomed he was asked by the American government to design both a light aircraft and a seaplane. Both designs were accepted and he concentrated on manufacturing them – and, as ever, innovating and improving the technology.

In 1921, ever the restless spirit, he virtually gave up on manufacturing both planes and bikes (though he did enter, and win, the Schneider cup twice in that decade) and became a property developer in Florida. In 1930, aged just 52, he died during what would now be entirely routine surgery following appendicitis. No-one seems to know how many Curtiss motorcycles were ever made, or when exactly their production was halted. There is a Glenn H Curtiss museum in his hometown of Hammondsport (Hammond was his middle name), where a whole range of his motorcycles are on display

IGNAZ SCHWINN: EXCELSIOR

Despite this publication being all about Harley-Davidsons, the name of Excelsior seems to crop up a number of times. You can't really look at Harley without considering its history (and the factory certainly wouldn't have it any other way!) and Excelsior was a serious rival during several key years of that history. In fact for a long time Excelsior was snapping at the heels of both H-D and Indian – right through until its demise as a motorcycle manufacturer in 1931.

Excelsior had been making bicycles and bicycle components since 1876 when it decided to add internal combustion power to its range. The first machine was produced in 1906 and was a single speed, single cylinder 21 cubic inch F-head, with both belt final drive and leading link suspension. It was good for about 35 mph and so was quite typical of the machines of the day. The factory

entered the bikes in reliability runs and won perfect 100% scores. In 1910 they followed the trend and launched a 61 ci V-twin. The single was discontinued three years later as the V-twin went up in capacity to 1,000 cc.

Meanwhile the Schwinn motorcycle company, one of the best known cycle manufacturers, had also been planning to enter the motorcycle market. At first Ignaz Schwinn intended to develop a completely new machine for his company to offer. As he looked around the marketplace though he realised that he was having to go a long way to beat the quality of what was already available, and so he decided to buy an existing company. He fixed his aim on Excelsior and bought the whole concern for a massive $500,000 in 1911.

Schwinn made it a priority for the marque to make its name in racing, where he soon had a heck of a lot going on. In the summer of that year racer Joe Wolters was setting speed records on the Excelsior V-twin. In the September Jake DeRoiser recorded a top speed of 94 mph, and by the end of the year Lee Humiston had hit 100 mph aboard an Excelsior at Playa del Ray in California.

In 1911 the V-twin cost just over $300 but Scwinn dropped the price to make the machine more competitive, and in 1912 it sold for $250. Speedsters could buy a race version of the bike (usually with the option of larger valves, among other refinements) directly from the factory for exactly the same price, which meant that privateers opted for Excelsiors and the name was often seen in the winners' enclosures across the country.

Schwinn's engineers made great advances in many crucial areas, such as efficient lubrication of the engine parts, and maintaining the correct alignment of the final drive belt. Schwinn created a factory race team and recruited some of the country's top riders, as well as putting his best engineers into the racing department. Working there must have been incredibly exciting, and the investment paid off. The only fly in the ointment was that Henderson was emerging as a very strong and annoying competitor. Schwinn knew what to do. He bought Henderson.

Ignaz Schwinn had been born in Germany in 1860 and had started building bicycles when they first became a real fashion item. He emigrated to the USA when he was 31 and found financial backing from a fellow German, Adolph Arnold, to begin manufacturing bicycles in Chicago's West Side. He was a tireless innovator, and in many ways was ahead of even Henry Ford in his pioneering use of mass construction techniques. By the turn of the century the company was building hundreds of thousands of bicycles a year. Schwinn saw the bicycles fad coming to an end long before several of his rivals, who went to the wall, and was very wise in moving across to motorcycles.

What was probably the very finest of the breed was unveiled in 1925, the Super-X. With a very solid and famously fast 45-degree V-twin engine displacing 750 cc, the bike could get within spitting distance of 70 mph, and was both comfortable and civilised. It cost $325. The Super-Xs of the late Twenties had glorious styling and were a very commercial proposition.

They really ought to have gone on to even greater things, but the crash of '29 left Schwinn almost bankrupt and brought an end to just about everything he had created. Ignaz's son, Frank, took over the business and decided to concentrate on the core bicycle business – a rare case of a motorcycle manufacturer going back to pedal power – and built up the

company once more. The business thrived and re-established itself as a very famous American brand. It finally went into liquidation in 2001 and the name has been bought and sold a couple of times since then.

ALBERT CROCKER

Crocker is one of the better known defunct American motorcycle marques, and is one that really ought to have survived. It's not difficult to imagine how the bikes would have evolved, and even how they might look today. The company never made a huge number of big bikes, and those large-capacity Crockers that still exist fetch very high prices. Paying over $100,000 for a Crocker is not unusual, and three years ago one sold at auction for $276,500 ... granted, it was the finest of the breed – a hemi-head V-twin – and as if that wasn't enough, it had been owned by one S. McQueen, actor...

Albert Crocker was born in 1882 and gained a degree in engineering before starting work at the Aurora Automatic Machine Company. Based in Aurora, Illinois, the company made the greatly respected Thor motorcycle. Al worked on the development of the Thor on weekdays and raced them at weekends. What a guy!

Al moved to Indian as a result of meeting Charles Hendee, and in 1924 – having married the widow of a fellow racer – he opened an Indian dealership in Kansas City. From there he moved on to establish an Indian dealership on Venice Boulevard in Los Angeles. In 1931 he began making 500 cc dirt track racers in small numbers, which

enjoyed huge success right from the start. From there it was probably inevitable that he would move on to road bikes.

Together with his colleague, Paul Bigsby, Al started designing a true superbike. He was absolutely intent on producing not just another motorcycle, but the very best bike on the road.

Al first offered his own make of motorcycle to discerning bikers in 1936. You didn't just walk into dealer showroom and buy one straight off the floor though; Al's philosophy was that the customer could order exactly the colour and spec – even down to the gear ratios – that he or she wanted, and so each machine would be bespoke. A great idea, but not the best business model in the world as it doesn't allow for mass production, and the machine was always going to be relatively expensive. Al offered his buyers a full refund if they weren't entirely happy with their purchase, and he was never – not even once – taken up on that offer

The Crocker was a terrific bike, and was ahead of what Harley and Indian were offering in many ways. The engine was a 61 cubic inch, 45-degree V-twin with hemispherical heads, and a compression ratio that could be specified at anything from 7:1 to a scary 11:1. The cylinder walls were made especially thick so that customers could have the company over-bore their engines up to capacities of 90 ci – a whopping 1,474 cc. This remained the biggest production motorcycle engine until Yamaha brought out the XV1600 in 1998.

Every aspect of the motor and transmission was made to handle huge power and massive torque. In standard trim the bikes put out around 60 horsepower, which was good for lightning acceleration and a top speed of around 110 mph.

Al also designed and built the Scootabout scooter, which was

an interesting departure for him. The Scootabout didn't use a home-made engine though; the motors were bought in from Lawson. It was a good looking and, as you'd expect, very well built machine. It had an art deco hint to its styling and it sold well. It was very popular with women, who were just beginning to ride two-wheeled machines in considerable numbers.

The outbreak of war brought the manufacture of Crockers – both small and large – to an end. Al could no longer get hold of the motors for the Scootabout as Lawson moved over to military production, and Crocker itself was turned over to military manufacturing (they made engine parts, mostly for Douglas). The last V-twin was made shortly after the USA entered the war.

Sadly Crocker did not re-start bike building after the war, and Al died in 1961, aged 74. His son, also called Albert, took over the running of the company.

It is said that the Crocker company made just 64 V-twins in all, which explains their high values today. It's not just Steve McQueen's example that's sold for a fortune; there are several other cases of good Crocker V-twins selling for well over $200,000. What a shame that Al didn't come back to bike production after 1945. There was obviously a market for high-end, personal-spec bikes, and the prosperous Fifties would have been a great time to be offering them to wealthy enthusiasts. In that he had a niche, he wouldn't have been in direct competition with H-D, and can you even start to imagine the sort of glories that Crocker would have on sale now?

ALBERT POPE

It's strange to think, but the period we're discussing here came only a couple of generations after the end of the American Civil War, and there would certainly have been people alive in the first couple of decades of the Twentieth century who remembered that conflict.

Lieutenant Colonel Albert Augustus Pope had served in the Union army during the war, and in the 1870s he started, firstly, importing bicycles, and then began manufacturing them. He was born in Boston, Massachusetts in 1843 into an old and well-connected family, but while he was still young his father saw the collapse of his business interests, and though Pope was well educated it was clear that he wasn't going to be a gentleman of leisure.

He volunteered for the Union army when he was 19 and was soon noted for his leadership, initiative and organisational abilities. He fought in several bloody battles and was promoted to Lieutenant Colonel when he was 22. After the war he went into business, firstly in footwear, but in 1877 he saw the commercial possibilities in the bicycling boom. He founded the Pope Manufacturing Company and as well as making bicycles he promoted their use by publishing a book, The Bicycler, and founding – at an initial cost of $60,000 – the magazine The Wheelman.

He used the brand name Columbia for his bicycles, and they sold extremely well. He didn't go into manufacturing motorcycles as early as you might think. His first use of power was the Pope-Tribune car, and after that he sold cars through several different brands. Albert Pope controlled factories in Ohio, Illinois, Connecticut and Indiana. The first

cars were electric powered and they too sold well. I've seen it written that in 1899 half of all the cars on America's roads were made by Pope, which – though not a large number in total – seems impressive.

It appears that Albert Pope had owned companies which built motorcycles from as early as 1903, but by the time the first Pope bike came out he was dead. The Pope business group got into financial trouble in 1908, perhaps through over-rapid expansion, and went out of Albert Pope's control that year.

In August 1909 the Washington Post reported, 'Colonel Albert A Pope, known as the father of bicycles in this country, and still more recently as one of the leading automobile manufacturers of the world, died at his summer home, Lindermere-by-the-Sea, late this afternoon. For more than a year Colonel Pope had been in rather poor health, during the troubles of his bicycle and automobile enterprises, which were forced into the hands of a receiver'. He was 66.

The name lived on though and motorcycle production was moved to Westfield in Massachusetts. The first Pope motorcycle – a single-cylinder machine – was unveiled in 1911. The following year they brought out a V-twin, which looked very much like what H-D was offering the public. The bike was capable of over 50 mph from the engine's 8 horsepower, and sold for what was then the average price for a large capacity bike, $250. Because Pope had built up a reputation for quality and reliability in their bicycles over the years, the Pope was very well received and sold in good numbers. It was a very worthy competitor for Harley and other manufacturers of mainstream V-twins.

The Pope V-twin was innovative in having overhead valves in its 45-degree, 61 cubic inch engine, and the pistons and con rods were carefully matched and balanced. The crankcases were made of an aluminium alloy, and the Armored Magneto electrics were remarkable for their reliability.

One aspect of the Pope which was truly impressive was the use of rear suspension. The system was effectively half of what we would come to know as 'plunger' suspension; the rear axle had about three inches of vertical movement on a rod which was fitted with a coil spring above the frame member. It was simple and effective, needed little maintenance, and was certainly innovative for the time.

The big Pope didn't change much during its production run. In its last year it went from belt final drive to chain, and could be bought either as a single-speed machine or with a three-speed gearbox. By then the engine had been improved to give 18 horsepower.

When the USA entered the First World War the Pope factory was required to turn over its manufacturing capacity to munitions (they made machine guns, at which Albert Pope would doubtless have excelled), and after the war they started making bicycles again but did not resume motorcycle production, which was a real shame.

JOSEPH MERKEL

Joseph Merkel was another of these hugely impressive pioneers crucial to the birth and evolution of the motorcycle, and who must have been truly remarkable men. Like so many others, he was inventive, innovative, resourceful and far-sighted. There must have been a lot of men like him, the majority unknown and unsung, in the development of the motor vehicle, and it's our great good fortune that so many of them saw the potential of putting an engine in between two wheels.

Born in 1872, Joe Merkel left school at 14 and started work in the engineering shop at the Michigan logging plant where his father worked. He had a sharp mind and was quick to learn, and there was no way that he was going to stay at the logging plant all his working life.

He was particularly skilled at machining and fabricating bespoke parts, and he was lucky enough to gain a place at what was then Michigan Agricultural College, and is now Michigan State University. He studied mechanical engineering, was absolutely in his element, and soaked up everything he was taught.

In 1897 he was working as a draughtsman in Wisconsin, but by the end of the century he had started his own company, selling his own bicycle parts. It's a now-familiar story, but within a few months of the birth of the Twentieth century Joe was bolting a simple, single-cylinder engine into a bicycle frame. He did the same with a tricycle, and might well have built the first internal combustion-powered vehicle in Wisconsin. If that it is the case then it's likely that William Harley knew about it and perhaps was even inspired by it.

He was soon offering motorcycles for sale, and by 1905 he was fielding a race team. As we've seen from these other early H-D rivals, winning races was the way to promote your brands and sell machines. Merkel machines saw great success. They were both fast and reliable; everything that both the racer and the road rider wanted.

The majority of early motorcycle manufacturers stuck with two-wheeled machines, but a small number of companies diversified into four wheels. The automobile was a logical next step for Joe, and in 1906 alone he sold 150 cars.

In 1909, running short of working capital, Joe sold his business to the Light Manufacturing Company, and two years later that was in turn bought by the Miami Cycle Manufacturing Company. Joe stayed with the business through both transactions and his brand name survived. The Miami company was based in a substantial red brick factory at 900-930 Grand Avenue, Middletown in Ohio (not in Miami at all) and sold bicycles and motorcycles using the Miami, Hudson and Raycycle names.

The Miami company dated from 1895, and had grown very quickly. By 1910 all of 1,000 people worked in the four storey premises, turning out 100,000 bicycles and 10,000 motorcycles each year. The reason for buying Merkel was to add a top end, prestige name to their range.

Joe was put to work building the very best machine he could, which must have been a commission from heaven for him. Freed of the difficulties of running a business, he had only to concentrate on engineering. The result was The Flying Merkel, which was the high point of Joe's motorcycle building career.

In 1914 The Flying Merkel won a national endurance record,

racing from Chicago to St Louis, ridden by Maldwyn Jones. Jones was a well-known dirt track racer who had accepted a job with Merkel as test rider. He continued racing while with the company, and though not officially backing him they did pay his expenses and provide whatever help he required. Jones experienced a lot of bad luck in his campaigns, but he was greatly respected, and his racing successes did a lot to publicise The Flying Merkel. On one occasion he won a five mile racer against a Mercer racing car on a dirt oval in Dayton, Ohio.

A couple of Joe's innovations were in the bike's suspension. He developed what we would now recognise as a mono-shock rear end, and he then coupled that with what was in effect telescopic suspension, using dual coil springs. Merkel forks stayed in use for many years after Merkel motorcycles had stopped production.

In 1914, in what turned out to be a prescient move, Joe sold his shares in the company and – with some money in the bank – continued his engineering career. He was granted yet more patents as he solved automotive problems. He patented the Merkel Motor Wheel, which was taken up by Indian. He then moved to Rochester, New York, and worked with the Cyclemotor company, developing their machines. At that time the road tax for motorcycles and cars in New York State was the same, and Joe took up the fight on behalf of the motorcyclist and succeeded in having the two-wheeled tax levels reduced.

Miami continued to make The Flying Merkel until 1917. It seems that Joe spent the rest of his life in Rochester, enjoying one of his other great passions – golf – and working for a wide range of charities. I haven't been able to find any record of when he died though.

In 1916, having lost Merkel's backing, Maldwyn Jones was quickly snapped up as test rider by … yes, Harley-Davidson.

GEORGE WYMAN: YALE

In 1903 the splendidly named Consolidated Manufacturing Company of Toledo, Ohio – makers of the Yale and Snell brands of bicycle – decided to get into the emerging motorcycle market. Rather than develop their own machines they bought up the California Motorcycle Company, and re-badged the machines as Yale-Californias.

These were fairly standard-looking bicycles with a 1.5 horsepower motor installed in the frame's cradle, just above the pedals. The 90 cc single cylinder lay along the diagonal front frame member, lying parallel with it.

The fuel tank was slung under the top rail and the ignition batteries were in a small box behind the rider's saddle. It was the most basic form of early motorcycle, simply a modified cycle, with everything added to the existing machine. They had originally been made in a factory at Folsom Street in San Francisco, California owned by one Roy Marks, who produced his first machine in 1901.

After the buy-out, a small number of modifications and improvements were made; the wooden wheels were replaced with spoked steel wheels, and a lubricator replaced the oil drip feed. There were minor improvements inside the engine and to the electrics, but that was about all. In 1905 the Yale-California gained a twist grip throttle, and the following year the word California was dropped and they were simply marketed as Yale motorcycles. The

bikes were lightweight, at 110 lbs, and sold for around $170. In their adverts the company said that their machine, '... was winning the deserved reputation of being the most satisfactory motorcycle on the market'.

So far so good – no great reason to get excited; these very modest machines were how just about all the earliest motorcycle pioneers started out, and to be honest most companies evolved a lot faster than Yale did.

The Yale-California could claim one huge prize though. In 1903 – yes, 1903 – it was the first motorcycle to be ridden across America from coast to coast.

George Adams Wyman was born in Oakland, California in 1877 and became a cycling fanatic in his teens. He moved to Australia because there was a more challenging competitive cycling scene there, but returned to the USA in 1902. He had made a name for himself in long distance bicycle runs and started to do the same with motorcycles. In 1902 he rode from San Francisco to Reno, Nevada – up over the Sierra Nevada mountains, and it was on that trip that he started to think about riding clear across the nation.

He began his journey in central San Francisco but timed it badly; Theodore Roosevelt had just become president and was visited Frisco, and the launch of George's epic trip received hardly any publicity in the local papers.

Imagine the sort of terrain George covered on his 3,600 mile journey! There were no highways as such, no interstates; for long distances he rode alongside the railway tracks – it wasn't always the most direct route but it was the safest and often the most level. The Yale-California offered very little in the way of power (we are talking about 1.5

horsepower, remember) and so he had to pedal up gradients of any severity, or at worst get off and push the machine.

The little bike did really rather well, in all fairness. It needed several stops for repairs along the way, and he got stuck in Chicago for several days when the crank broke. By the time he was reaching the eastern seaboard it really was wearing out though, and he had to pedal the last 150 miles as the engine had completely given up the ghost. George wore a three-piece tweed suit with a shirt and tie for the trip, and when he arrived in New York City (and for some time after) his hands had to be bandaged from hanging onto the handlebar grips for so long. He reached NYC in the late summer, and by August had returned to San Francisco (with the bike) by train.

Yale made great play of his achievement in their publicity material but in fact the bike wasn't a Yale-California at all, but a California – having been made just before the take-over. Our hero lived to be 82, dying in California in 1959.

Yale finally began to catch up with motorcycle fashions, bringing out larger and more sophisticated bikes from about 1910. In 1912 they brought out a 998 cc V-twin with chain final drive which was good for around 55 mph. It had a very handsome engine with sharply-cut horizontal fins and a smart two-into-one exhaust. One feature of their bikes was a bolt-on rear section for a pillion passenger which seated the passenger behind the centre of the rear wheel. The front wheel must hardly ever have been on the ground. Yale made its last bike in 1915, but to this day its one great claim to fame is George Wyman's amazing, pioneering ride across the USA. **SM**

Words: Steven Myatt
Photos: Bob Clarke
Archive Photos: Corbis

The last American hero

Robert Craig Knievel was born on October 17 1938 in Butte, Montana, and died on November 30 2007, aged 69. And it's absolutely remarkable that he made it to within spitting distance of his allotted three score years and ten. If you sold life insurance he was the last man you'd ever ask to put a signature to a policy. Robert Craig – better known as Evel, of course – could have died during any one of the thousands of motorcycle stunts he performed during his career. Amazingly he didn't; in fact, he was taken away by pulmonary fibrosis, not a fall from a great height.

There have been many other stunt riders since, but he remains the by-word for a real showman; a man who made motorcycles do things which they were very definitely not designed to do.

Robert Craig was born to Robert and Ann Knievel, his father being of German extraction. When he was just two years old his parents separated and both left the area, leaving Robert Craig to be brought up by his father's parents, Ignatius and Emma Knievel. Despite this, he seems to have had a happy childhood. Butte was a blue collar mining town when he was young, and as a teenager he rapidly gained a local reputation as an excellent athlete.

After finishing his schooling, he got a job driving an earth mover for a local copper-mining company, and distinguished himself by driving into a power cable and blacking out the town. In his teens he showed signs of being something of a rebel – and a dare-devil. He had been taken to his first stunt show by his grandparents when he was just eight, and in later life he always credited this as his first inspiration. ▶

Left: In his heyday Evel cut a very glamorous figure. He was a modern-day adventurer in an age which was becoming increasingly cosseted. It's fair to say that he adored fame.

Above: Harley-Davidson's XR-750 was Evel's jump bike of choice for many years. He enjoyed a very close relationship with the factory.

That show, he recalled, was headed by Joie Chitwood, a Cherokee Indian from Texas, who had made his name as a dirt-track racer, and went on to a very successful career in Indy car racing. His 'Thrill Shows' toured for forty years, and starred the infamous 'Hell Drivers'. Joie died in Florida in 1988, aged 75,

He acquired his first motorcycle thanks to his father. Bob E Knievel had moved to Berkeley in California and started a new life there and re-married. He worked on Volkswagen cars and Robert often visited him. On one occasion, when he was fifteen, his father presented him with a BSA Bantam. It was a tiny, 125 cc two-stroke, but Robert loved it.

To the delight and amazement of the crowd, Evel lined up his bike, rode towards the ramp and took off. So far, so good.

It seems that Robert Craig had a few minor brushes with the local police, and on one occasion, when he was eighteen, he was arrested after crashing his motorbike. It was during that overnight stay in jail that he acquired his nickname. In an adjoining cell was a man called William Knofel, who the officer called Awful Knofel. He then extended the rhyming theme by called Robert Craig Evil Knievel. Robert Craig liked it and decided to keep it, but changed the spelling to Evel to avoid giving offence.

Having said that, Evel did have another version of how he got his nickname. This says that he and his brother stole the hubcaps off a car owned by a local baseball umpire, one Nate McGrath, and he called him Evil. Which, again, got changed to Evel because the connotations of the alternative were a bit too much, even for him. You believe whichever version you prefer.

Evel started to channel his energies into both rodeo shows and semi-professional ski-jumping competitions. In 1957, he won the Northern Rocky Mountain Ski Association championships. Soon afterwards he joined the US Army, serving in the infantry and excelling as both a pole vaulter and a hurdler.

At the end of the decade, having left the military and returned to Butte, he married local girl Linda Joan Bork. They were to be together for 38 years and have four children in all, and even after their divorce they remained very close.

At this point he saw his future being as a professional athlete, playing hockey. It was very competitive though, and what cash he got to take home was very limited. Then Evel's entrepreneurial spirit started to show. Evel started a local semi-pro hockey team, the Butte Bombers. He described himself as its 'owner, general manager and player/coach' and was involved with it for a couple of years. That lead to a scandal though, when the takings were found to have been stolen after the Bombers played the Czechoslovakian Olympic team. As he had been sent off the pitch during the game, Evel was a suspect, but nothing was proved, and the American Olympic Committee ended up paying the Czech guests' expenses.

His next project ended with police attention too. He set himself up as a guide for hunters and fishermen who were visiting the Montana mountains, and guaranteed his clients that they would always see a great catch with him. In fact, he was taking them into the adjoining Yellowstone national park, where the game was protected by law, and his activities constituted poaching.

By the early Sixties he was competing in motocross but a spill put him in hospital, and needing to put food in his family's stomachs

AN EVEL TRIBUTE - IN MORE WAYS THAN ONE!

Now, here's something rather more than slightly different: Dutchman Jitze Van Der Vinne has been a fan of Evel Knievel for as long as he can remember, so it surprised no-one when he decided to build a bike by way of a tribute to his hero.

It wasn't going to be a replica of one of his jump bikes though; no, something far more modern. Yep, and faster. He had a big bore Sportster engine lying around that had been worked over by Zipper's Performance Cycles, and he decided to drop it into a Streetfighter frame. There are lots of custom frame builders in Holland, but he decided to look across the English Channel, and ordered a bespoke chassis from British master craftsmen Spondon.

He added an Ohlins rear swing arm and a pair of Showa front forks

from A Honda SP1. The billet wheels came from PVM, and the four-pot callipers are Nissin items, while the callipers are by Brembo. Jitze made up the yokes himself, and the seat unit and the exhaust system (think loud, by the way – as if you hadn't guessed). The fuel tank and the rear-sets are Spondon items, as you would expect. The paintwork, a fairly exact replica of Evel's favourite colour scheme, was laid on by Hugo Brabant of Uden in Holland – and it's just right.

However, there was a reason why Evel used to jump on bikes with smooth-topped tank and seat units. You really would not want to try a jump on this beast, now would you? I don't need to paint a picture of how that great hump-backed tank might damage a man's groin at high speed, do I?

---

he made the unlikely switch to selling insurance. He seemed to be doing very well in his new post, though it did transpire that he had been signing up inmates at the local asylum for expensive policies. Once again under something of a cloud he left Butte, and took his family to Moses Lake in Washington. Here he set up a motorcycle dealership in partnership with a guy named Darell Triber, with the local Honda franchise, but despite his best endeavours – which included offering a $100 dollar discount on a new bike to anyone who could beat him at arm wrestling – the business failed.

Evel quickly got a job working for another dealer, Jim Pomeroy, who he knew from motocross racing (Evel was riding a Norton scrambler at the time). It was Jim who taught him basic bike stunts, such as pulling wheelies and riding while standing on the saddle. Evel was a natural, and he was soon out-classing his tutor and devising new stunts.

He was quickly reminded of the stunt show

12 CRUCIAL EVEL KNIEVEL FACTS

Born	Died
1938	2007

Number of wives
2

Number of sons
2

Number of daughters
2

Cost of the Skycycle
$150,000

Heat in the Skycycle engines
3,000° F

Favourite bike
Harley XR-750

Best one-off audience
90,000

Favourite tipple before jumps
Wild Turkey bourbon

Number of broken bones
35

Inducted into the Motorcycle Hall Of Fame
1999

he had seen all those years ago, and he had one of those blinding flashes of inspiration so beloved of cartoonists. The bulb lit up and it was a lot of watts. Evel was going to be a stunt rider, but perhaps as importantly he decided that he was going to be his own promoter. He wasn't going to be a mere journeyman, a hired hand just bought in for the day; he was going to organise everything and go home with the profits at nightfall.

He lost no time. He found a venue and did a deal to hire it, he organised the publicity and arranged the adverts. On the day he sold the tickets at the gate and then took to the microphone to introduce himself. He did a few of the basic tricks that he'd learned from Jim, and then lined up for his first professional jump.

He had set up a home-made wooden box about 25 feet long. In it was a curious mix of two mountain lions (borrowed from an obliging zoo, it's said) and a large number of locally sourced rattlesnakes. Interesting. This was what he was going to jump. It's not hard ▶

to spot the showman in all this, is it?

To the delight and amazement of the – small, it must be said – crowd, Evel lined up his bike, rode towards the ramp and took off. So far, so good. As he was to say in later life, it's not the jump that's the problem, it's the landing. And he landed short. His back wheel dropped into the far end of the pit, but to the disappointment of the crowd he wasn't eaten by the lions or bitten by the snakes, and he was able to take a standing ovation with his dignity and his limbs intact. It is said that the falling bike shattered the wooden side of the casing and the rattlesnakes were released into the crowd. That might have been true, but if it wasn't then it was certainly a detail that Evel could have added himself.

The one-man show hadn't lasted very long though, and Evel realised that while he couldn't certainly make a go of this, he did need to pad out the performance. He needed to create a bigger attraction.

Evel went to see Bob Blair, who had a Norton dealership in California, and they agreed that Bob's company would sponsor the run of events. It was a good deal for both of them; it gave Bob's business the right sort of exposure, and Evel got the funds he needed to put on a real show. The first performance took place on January 3, 1966 at the National Date Festival at Indio in California – south-east of Los Angeles and a few miles west of the Joshua Tree national park.

The following month he organised a show at Barstow, in the desert, north-east of LA. He tried out a new stunt, in which he jumped over a bike which was running towards him at speed. He left it just a little too late though and the bike hit him. He was thrown into the air and hit the ground hard. Just a month later he was back at the same venue in front of a crowd, finishing the act.

We can only shake our heads in amazement, whistle through our teeth in awe, and admire the man

---

That incident had put him in hospital though, and while there his newly recruited group broke up, so, pragmatically, he went back to performing stunts on his own, turning up at any event that would include him. He was slowly building up a reputation as a dare-devil rider, and with his flair for self-publicity he never lost an opportunity to promote himself. In June '66, back up in Montana, he failed to clear the final vehicle while jumping over twelve cars and a van, and broke his arm and a number of ribs. He turned that crash into a positive though, using his injuries – and his rapid return to riding – to further enhance his image.

Almost exactly a year later he had another fairly serious accident. This time he was jumping sixteen cars and a van, and crashed and suffered concussion. As ever he swore that he would return and finish the show. Two months later, in August '67, he did indeed return, but he crashed yet again – albeit in front of an even larger crowd. This time he

shattered his right knee, left wrist and two of his ribs.

Later that year Evel engineered what was, despite the stunt's failure, his big breakthrough. He arranged to jump over the fountains at Caesar's Palace in Las Vegas. As you'd expect in Vegas, there was huge razzmatazz around the jump, and Evel had paid out of his own pocket to have it filmed, having already agreed with ABC that they would screen it if it looked good. The date set for the jump was New Year's Eve 1967. He was 29 years old.

He did jump the fountains, but something went wrong. He slid down the far ramp and fell onto the asphalt of the parking lot. This time he broke his hip, both ankles, one leg and one wrist, and crushed his pelvis. As he later said, 'That was the most serious crash of them all. I landed on my head. There was a little six-foot safety ramp and I landed on top of it. It was a horrible jump; I just wasn't going fast enough.'

On the up-side, ABC put the film of the crash on television and that gave him nationwide exposure, as well as bringing in a lot of money for the rights to its screening.

Although the doctors told him that he might never walk unaided again, Evel cashed in on his fame by announcing his intention to jump the Grand Canyon. A mere five months after the Vegas crash though, he failed to jump fifteen Ford Mustangs in Scottsdale, Arizona and broke a foot and a leg. Once again he spent as little time convalescing as possible; although he suffered injury like any other mortal when his body hit immovable objects, he seemed to have super-human powers of recovery. Part of that might have been physical, but a lot was certainly down to his determination. Mind over matter.

Evel was working very hard to turn himself into a celebrity, indeed, into a brand name. He had long, wavy hair and the sideburns appropriate to the period, he wore custom-made jump suits, and carried a gold cane – which wasn't just a prop; he really needed that to be able to walk. His clothes and his helmets were always just right for a barn-storming showman; nothing could be too flashy. That extended to his motorcycles too; the tools of his trade. During most of the Sixties he used Triumph Bonneville T120s for his stunts, but – never one to miss an opportunity to make a dollar – he asked Triumph to pay him for using them. They refused absolutely, and he approached Harley, who were delighted to sponsor him. It was a very fitting tie-up, and as soon as it came out in 1970 the XR-750 Sportster racer fell into his hands and quickly become synonymous with his name. Painted red, white and blue, and with all bright-work highly polished, the powerful but lightweight XR was the perfect mount for an all-American dare-devil.

Years later he said, 'I was with Harley-Davidson for eight years and they treated me wonderfully. They were a first-class company, and they have been good to me all through the years. They kept their word with me, they treated me right, and they stood behind me.'

Ever the businessman, Evel was never slow to get into merchandising. He sold posters, T-shirts, hats – anything that would reinforce the marketing, as well as bring in a few more bucks. He also licensed his name and image to third parties, and a whole range of Evel Knievel products became available. Evel didn't hang about. He had

Both tests failed to get to the far side, but Evel shrugged off the failures and said that the jump would go ahead as planned

He once said, 'All Elvis ever did was stand on a stage and play guitar. He never fell off on that pavement at no eighty miles an hour'

found his commercial niche and was very good at finding all the extra angles. He made a lot of money, but then he spent it very freely too. He was extravagant in everything he did.

Strangely, he wasn't very popular with American bikers. You would have thought that he'd have been a real figure of note in this area; a counter-culture hero for the late Sixties and Seventies. The trouble was that he had opinions which ran counter to the majority and wasn't backward in expressing them. He was very much in favour of legislation to make the wearing of crash helmets compulsory, and he lectured one and all at length about what he saw as the evils of drink and drugs.

In this he was somewhat like Elvis, who also spoke out against drugs – even, famously, being appointed to a vacuous anti-drugs post by Richard M Nixon. All hypocrisy, of course. Elvis was no stranger to drug use. Similarly, Evel was fond of a drink – indeed he finally admitted that he took a good measure of bourbon before every jump – and he also had a problem with addiction to pain-killers (which is entirely understandable, I guess).

Evel liked parallels with Elvis, and he considered himself to be The King's equal as a showman and entertainer. He once said, 'All Elvis ever did was stand on a stage and play guitar. He never fell off on that pavement at no eighty miles an hour'.

He kept promoting the notion of a jump over the Grand Canyon, but the site is government property and they were never going to

allow it to open. The unique landscape was worth more to them that Evel's ambitions. He considered several alternatives, including the Mississippi river and – he can't have been serious about this one – a jump from one New York skyscraper to another. Eventually he decided that a good alternative was the Snake River Canyon, near Twin Falls in Idaho. He announced that he would perform the jump on September 4 – Labour Day – 1972.

Things had been going pretty well. He had sold 100,000 tickets for his run of jumps at the Houston Astrodome, and in Ontario, California he had successfully jumped nineteen cars. He'd had his spills though – fractures were becoming quite routine. At Daly City in California he fell off the XR-750 and it ran over him, causing concussion and breaking his back. That was nothing; three months earlier he had broken both of his legs, his right arm and his collar bone.

He went on to jump over thirteen buses – and shatter his pelvis – at the Wembley Stadium in London, in front of 90,000 people (though the advance publicity had given the impression that they were to ➤

Above: Snake River Canyon
Right: The launch looked good...
Right Top: ...But ended in failure after a drone chute deployed too soon and Evel plummeted to the riverbank.

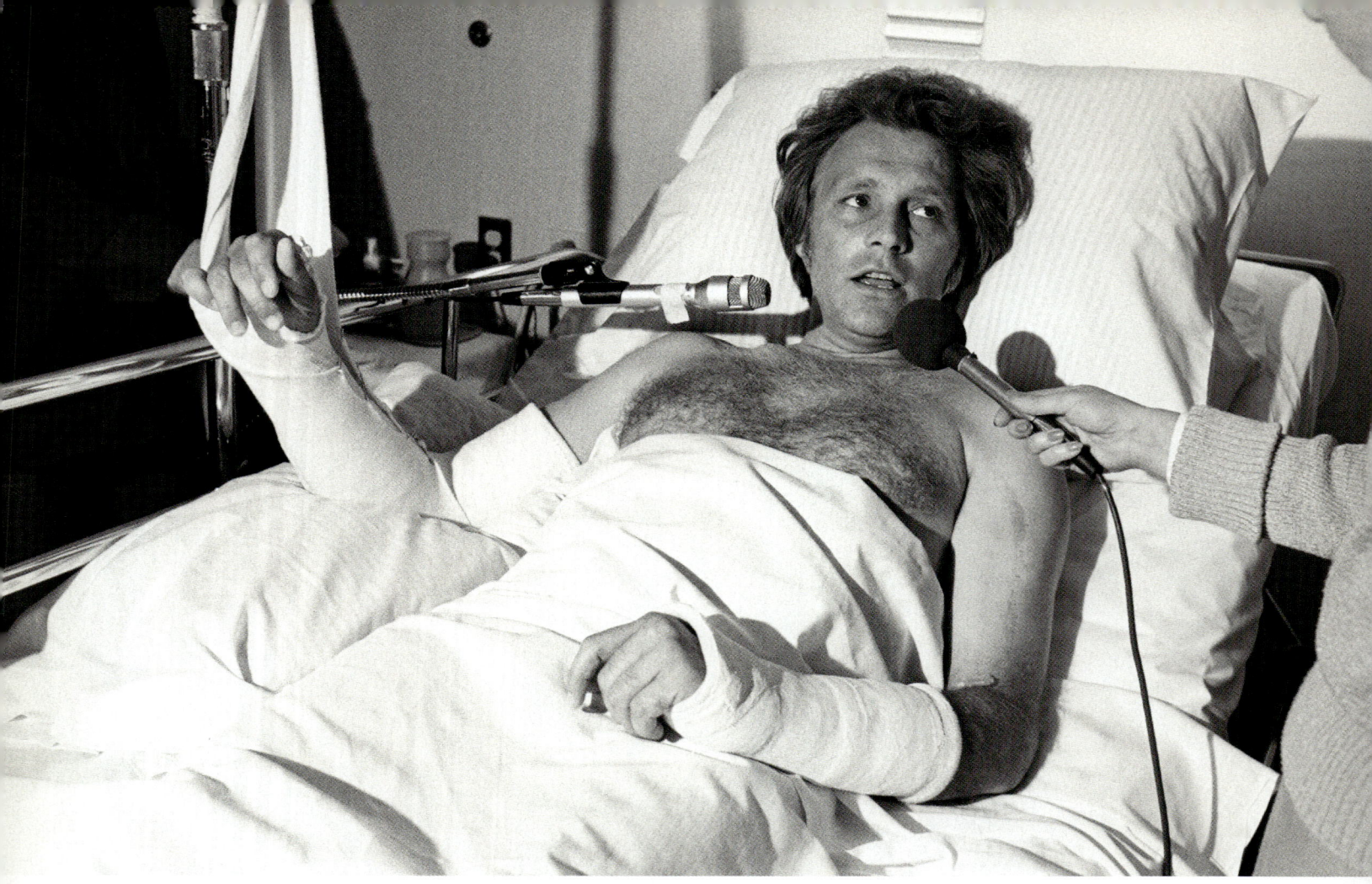

Although the doctors told him that he might never walk unaided again, Evel cashed in on his fame by announcing his intention to jump the Grand Canyon

be double decker buses, which they were not). In Ohio he jumped fourteen Greyhound buses. In Canada he sailed over thirteen Mack trucks, and in Yakima, Washington he successfully cleared thirteen Pepsi-Cola delivery trucks. He crashed again in Chicago while jumping over a tank of sharks; a piece of metal flying from the crashing bike cost a cameraman an eye.

It has to be said that he was a man of amazing courage. Either that or he was utterly unconcerned by his frequent injuries. If any one of us had suffered even one of his crashes we would probably never have gone back for another dose of the medicine. Not so Evel. He could never wait to get out of the hospital, into one of his exuberant leather jump suits, and back onto an XR. He must have known that bad

crashes were going to happen again ... and again, but nothing could stop him. He must have known that being paralysed or brain damaged was a very real possibility; a fate which, for him, probably would have been worse than death. We can only shake our heads in amazement, whistle through our teeth in awe, and admire the man.

In the early Seventies he had commissioned the building of a jet-powered bike, named the X-1 Skycycle, as a demonstration of his intent rather than as a functioning, viable machine. Now he had the X-2 built, and tested it twice at the jump site at Snake River Canyon. Both times it failed to get to the far side, but Evel shrugged off the failures and said that the jump would go ahead as planned. And it did. And it wasn't a success.

The force generated by take-off caused the bolts on the cover over the parachute to snap off, and the chute deployed instantly. Instead of gliding across the river and coming down gently on the other side, the chute trailing behind it, the bike was pulled up short. It fell onto the river bank and came to rest half in and half out of the water. Evel was bruised but otherwise unhurt. Technically it wasn't a glorious day, but the showman managed to use the occasion to further enhance and extend his reputation. And he made money, that's for sure; it's said that he took away $3 million dollars, which thirty five years ago was quite a pay day.

In the Seventies two movies were made about him. How could a movie not have been made about such a maverick and larger-than-life character? The first, which premiered in 1971, was The Evel Knievel

Opposite: Evel being interviewed in his hospital bed after yet another crash
Above: Not long before he died our contributor Bob Clarke caught up with Evel and reported him to be on good form. The bike was a special commemorative machine made for him by CMC

documentary fronted by Richard Hammond – who failed to get a useful word out of the great man. Evel made a guest appearance as himself on the TV show The Bionic Woman.

One of the most infamous incidents in his life occurred in 1977 after a book, Evel Knievel On Tour, was written by Shelly Saltman. Saltman was a senior executive at Twentieth Century Fox and had worked as promoter for the Snake River jump, and in the book he had allegations about Evel's drinking and drug taking. Evel and an associate found Saltman and beat him senseless with a baseball bat. He was very badly hurt and endured a series of operations, Evel was charged with the assault and was sentenced to six months in jail and three years probation. He showed no remorse, and treated the whole thing as one long publicity stunt.

Saltman then took out a civil suit for damages and was awarded $13 million, though it is said that he never received so much as a cent. As a result of the action though, the tax inspectors took a close look at Evel's affairs. They claimed that he had been evading income tax for years, and demanded $1.6 million by way of back payments, and $2.5 million in interest and fines. The files were passed on to the state authorities and Montana asked for $390,000 in unpaid state taxes. Evel declared himself bankrupt.

By now his glory days were over, but he carried on with most of his old, high-living ways – though he did start playing golf too. He had made his last professional jump at Hollywood, Florida in March 1981. Linda left him after he was accused of soliciting an undercover policewoman. He was later found guilty of illegal possession of firearms. In 1995 he picked up a number of traffic tickets in Florida, including one – ironically – for not having a driving licence.

There were two highlights in his final years; he became a born-again Christian, and he began painting – mostly horses and religious themes. Both gave him great satisfaction, and the second brought him some income when he sold prints of his work.

By now he had been diagnosed with Hepatitis C, probably contracted during a blood transfusion following one of his innumerable crashes. He was in constant pain from his old injuries and his movement was becoming severely restricted. In 1999, he married his girlfriend Krystal Kennedy but the marriage lasted less than two years. He had hip replacement surgery and an emergency liver transplant.

He died in Clearwater, Florida, and was buried back home in Butte. The town had always been enormously proud of their famous son, whatever his imperfections. They had inaugurated an annual Evel Knievel Day by way of a civic party, and their hero was given a splendid send-off. And a hero is exactly what he was. **SM**

Story. It starred George Hamilton, with Sue Lyon as his wife. Evel sold them his own footage of some of his most famous jumps.

Later in the decade he starred as himself – alongside Gene Kelly, most implausibly – in Viva Knievel. In the movie, he plays a stunt man performing in Mexico who out-wits a gang of drug dealers intent on smuggling cocaine into the USA inside his coffin (except, of course, he doesn't die ...). Absolute hokum.

His life was re-visited in the 2004 film Evel Knievel with George Eads (who plays Nick in CSI) and Jaime Pressly (from My Name Is Earl, and any number of films) as Evel and Linda. The following year, already in poor health, he collaborated with a documentary about his life. Just months before he died he was the subject of a BBC TV

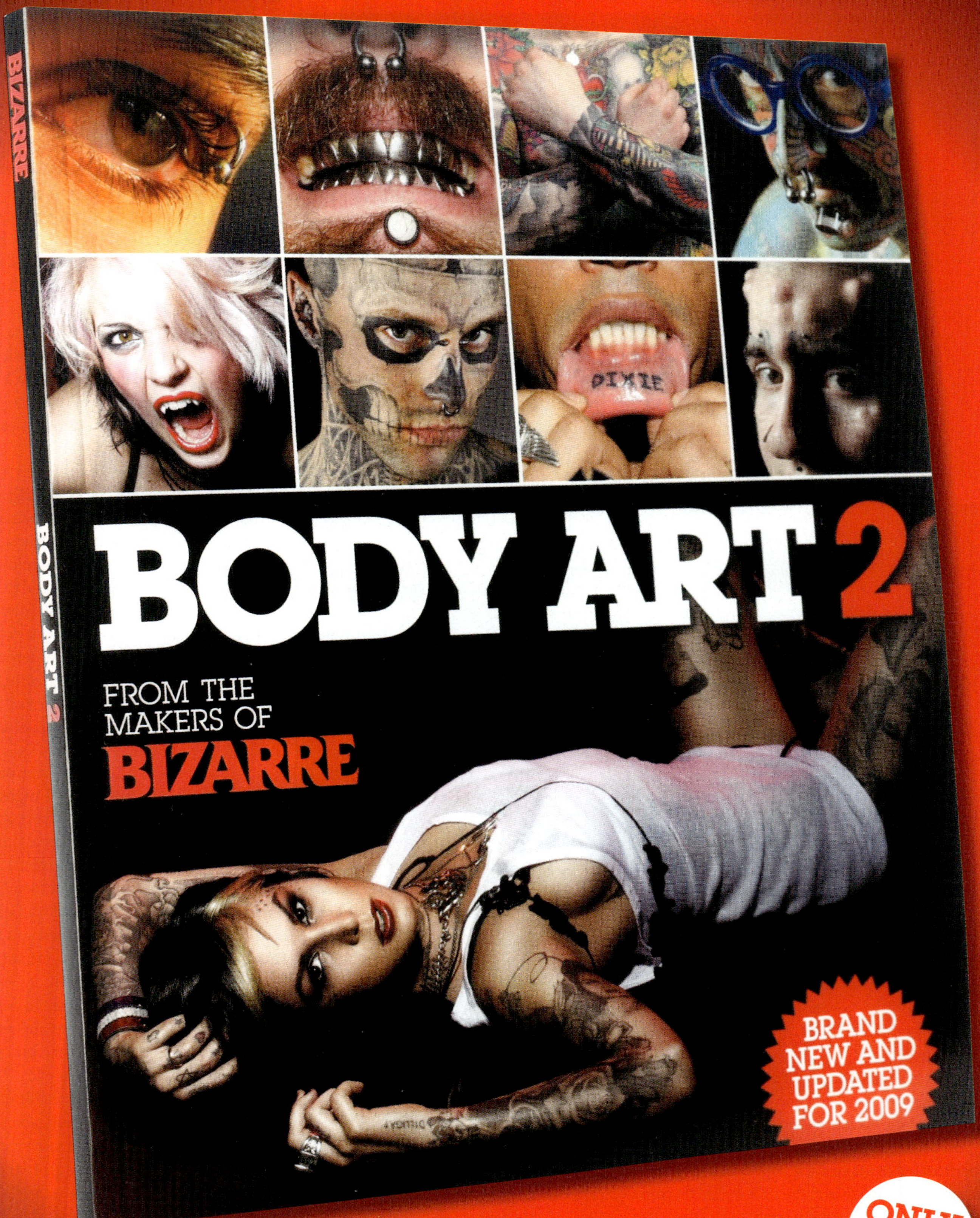

105
ESSENTIAL FACTS ABOUT HARLEYS

Words: Steven Myatt

001 The very first Harleys were painted black, but from 1906 grey was an option. The colour used was a Renault shade, until the company introduced their own grey in 1910.

002 The Servi-Car was introduced in 1932, and one intended use was that it would be towed behind a new car so that the delivery driver could ride away, leaving the car with its new owner (the Servi-Car being equipped with a tow bar at the front).

003 An electric starter was fitted to the Servi-Car as standard in 1964, making it the first self-starting Harley.

004 Thanks to military demand the factory produced 26,708 bikes in 1918, but only 3,703 in 1933 (due to the economic depression).

005 Production in 1941 was a huge 52,891 thanks to orders placed by the various military agencies.

006 Harley's 21-FS model was manufactured in 1921 but was only ever sold in Britain – and then not until 1922.

007 The Knucklehead engine was introduced in 1936 and the factory anticipated a run of 1,600 machines that year. In fact they sold only 152 – and just 126 the following year.

008 The Panhead engine and telescopic front forks were both first introduced in 1948.

009 Harley-Davidson began supporting muscular dystrophy charities in 1980, and since then has raised more than $65 million to help combat the disease.

010 At the time of the company's 100th anniversary in 2005, the Harley Owners' Group had 660,000 members in 115 countries.

011 Big Twins were available with hand gear-change and foot clutches between 1952 and 1978 but only 200 machines were ever sold with that option each year.

012 From 1912 the 'fully floating' saddle was offered, with twin springs at the back of the saddle and a coil spring inside the frame's central upright tube.

013 Although electric lighting was offered on World War One era bikes, many riders opted for acetylene-powered headlights and tail lights. These were fed from a tank mounted on the bike's handle bars.

014 The 1907 Harley-Davidson cost $210 new (with tools, tool holder and tyre repair kit). That year a blue collar worker in the USA earned around 22 cents an hour, giving him an average annual income of $400. So the bike would cost just over six months pre-tax income.

015 In 1927 the factory introduced the lightweight, single-cylinder BA model. The capacity was just 21 cubic inches (344cc). It ran for a decade but never sold in great numbers.

016 In the 1920s 'bootleg' Harleys – which the company thought were being shipped to Mongolia – were on sale illicitly in Japan.

017 Race ace Joe 'Smokin' Joe' Petrali got his first Harley ride in 1925 when rider Ralph Hepburn crashed and injured his hand. Joe (previously a rider for Indian) stepped out of the crowd, took over and won.

018 In 1960 Harley introduced the 165cc Topper scooter. It had automatic transmission and a lawn mower-style recoil starting system.

019 The FXB Sturgis – introduced in 1982 – was named after the famous biker meet in South Dakota, of course, but feature, a toothed rubber final drive belt – something not seen for many years.

020 If you opt for the 'Fly And Ride' option of H.O.G. membership, you can arrive anywhere in the USA, Canada, Europe, and Australia, go to a Harley dealer and collect a bike and ride off. You have to give it back eventually though.

021 The shed in which the first Harleys were made was preserved until the Seventies, when some external contractors cleared it away by mistake.

022 In 2007, the company generated 73.5% of its revenue in the USA, 13.8% in Europe, 4% in Japan, 4% in Canada and 4.7% in other territories.

023 The beautiful and tough-looking XLCR was introduced in 1977 as a rival to the increasingly fast sports bikes coming in from Japan. Unfortunately they were cheaper and faster and the XLCR was only in production for two years.

024 Going heavy on the retro theme, the Softail-framed FXSTS model of 1988 used springer front forks – not seen since telescopic forks were introduced forty years before. And it handled better than you'd have thought.

025 Flathead-engined bikes come with 45ci, and 61 or 74 ci motors. They look very much the same, but the way to tell them apart is that the drive chain on the 45 is on the right, and the left on its larger-engined siblings.

026 Even after the Knucklehead engine was introduced, the company sold bikes powered by the obsolete Flathead motor for many years. It was discontinued for two-wheel use in 1948.

027 Ex-H-D man Erik Buell founded his sports bike manufacturing company in 1987. The bikes were always powered by Harley engines and H-D completed its gradual buy-out of Buell in 2003, making it a wholly-owned subsidiary.

028 Bill Davidson was just 21 when he designed his first motorcycle in 1901.

029 In 2007, an agreement was reached between H-D and the Indian Ministry for Industry and Commerce. As a result, Harley-Davidson motorcycles are now on sale in India. In exchange India can export mangoes to the USA. Honestly!

030 In 1932 a Servi-Car cost $450 new. In 1942 the price had gone up to $510 for the base model. By '52 is was nearly twice that at $1,047, and by '62 a Servi-Car would have set you back $1,523. But then, inflation of 300% over 30 years doesn't seem so bad.

031 In relatively recent times, the lowest sale of any one model in a given year was the XLR in 1959. Just five of the race-orientated Sportsters were sold.

032 In 1965 H-D sold a record 6,930 Electra-Glides.

033 Bikes sold to police departments in the US came in exclusive colours not available to the public. Before WW2 this was usually blue, but after 1945 also silver.

034 Harley kept the launch price of its bikes at $210 until 1911, when the base price of a 7D was $300.

035 The earliest prototype Harley went fine on the flat but wasn't powerful enough to go up hills of almost any gradient.

036 Harley discontinued its two-stroke machines in 1978 after pressure from the Environmental Protection Agency, which voiced concerns about emissions from these engines.

037 The average age of new Harley owners in the States is increasing year by year. In 2003 it was just under 45; by 2007 it was 48. 15% of the total were buying their first ever motorcycle.

038 Unless specified otherwise, police Panheads came with a two-way radio in the left-hand saddlebag and an exposed brass fire extinguisher on top of the right.

039 The first Fat Bob was named after Robert J Gruzzmann who works in the welding shop at the factory.*

040 Co-founder of the Motor Maids, Linda Dugeau, first rode a Harley in 1932. She travelled all over the States and wrote about her journeys for Motorcyclist magazine.

041 In November 2006 at a charity auction in Doha, Qatar, a VRSCDX Night Rod Special was sold for $800,000. The money raised went to UNESCO and the buyer was Sheikh Tamim, the Crown Prince of Qatar.

042 The 1984 FXRT was remarkable in that it had the new and, for Harley, quite revolutionary Evo engine, rubber mounts for the motor, and a five-speed gearbox. Damn nice bike too.

043 The 1965 FL Electra-Glide weighed more than 700 lbs; a hell of a lot for the time. A 2008 FLHTCU Ultra Classic Electra Glide weighs 814 lbs.

044 When the Sportster was introduced, its drive chain and gear lever were on the right; the opposite of the set-up on the Big Twins. This was because the Sportster was in competition with light, fast British bikes which also had this arrangement.

045 The pretty XLCH Sportster introduced in 1959 was the first 'street scrambler', intended for off- as well as on-road riding.

046 In 1955, a go-faster kit was available for the KH. This cost $68 and raised the designation to KHK.

047 In the late Forties, both Harley and BSA bought the rights to manufacture DKW's two-stroke, 3 bhp, 125cc machine (as part of the post-war reparations scheme). At first H-D called it the Model S, then re-named it the Hummer. No relation to the huge 4x4 of the same name.

048 Servicemen from Britain, Russia and China rode Harleys during WW2, as well as Americans.

049 After Indian went out of business in 1953, Harley-Davidson was left as the sole American motorcycle manufacturing company.

050 In August 2008, H-D bought 100% of Italian bike manufacturer MV Agusta for 70 million euro ($108 million at that point), including uplifted debt. The deal included the Cagiva name as well as Agusta.

051 The cheapest Harley in the USA in 2008 was the Sportster XL 883 at $6,695. The FLHTCU Ultra Classic Electra Glide was $20,695. The UK prices were £5,195 and £16,995 – making the big tourer the better value of the two!

052 Harley's best year of the Fifties and Sixties was 1966, when they sold 36,320 machines. The worst year was 1963, with just 9,873 bikes sold.

053 When the company was incorporated in 1906, Walter Davidson was named as President, Arthur Davidson was Sales Manager and Secretary, William Davidson was Vice President and Factory Manager, and Bill Harley was Chief Engineer and Treasurer.

054 The 1952, K Model could turn the quarter mile in about 16.8 seconds at around 53 mph, and had a top speed of just over a 100 mph.

055 During the AMF years, H-D's design department worked on a 4-cylinder, liquid-cooled motor (with radiators hidden beneath the seat and under side covers) code-named Nova. It never made it into production.

056 The XR-750 dirt-track racer was capable of around 130 mph in the right hands, and sold for a very reasonable $5,000 considering it was such a specialist machine.

057 The company celebrated its fiftieth anniversary in 1954 with a startling Anniversary Yellow FL Hydra-Glide. It had a commemorative medallion on its front mudguard and a trumpet horn.

058 Steve McQueen's 1929 Harley-Davidson Model B was sold at auction in 2006 (along with two of his Indians). Auctioneers Bonham's got $32,000 for it against a guide price of $14-16,000. A Harley bicycle poster of his went for $500 against a lowest guide price of $50.

059 Warr's of London is Europe's oldest Harley-Davidson dealers, having been founded in 1924.

060 The new frame offered on the JD model in 1925 had the seat set a full three inches lower than on the previous year's model.

061 The 1961 Harley-Davidson Sprint was powered by a four-stroke 250cc Aermacchi engine imported from Italy. The CR250 flat track racer was based on the Sprint and enjoyed considerable success,

062 Harley-Davidson has a 1956 KH once owned by Elvis Presley on display at the museum in Milwaukee. The Gracelands museum has four more ex-Elvis Harleys.

063 H-D purchased full control of Aermacchi's motorcycle production in 1974.

064 In 1993, the company introduced the FLSTN Heritage Softail, which was nicknamed – a little unfortunately – the Cow Glide. It was black and white and had a heifer-skin seat. H-D sold 2,700 of them.

065 Unless specified otherwise, Servicars came with three forward gears and one reverse gear.

066 Willie G Davidson's middle name is Garibaldi.**

067 Graceland Harley-Davidson dealership opened in January 2007 at 3727 Elvis Presley Boulevard, Memphis Tennessee.

068 In 1914, Harley boasted that their Model 11-F was the first motorcycle that could climb a 60 degree incline.

069 In 1948, anticipating post-war demand, Harley opened a large, new engine-building plant at Wauwatosa in Wisconsin – to the west of the main Milwaukee factory.

070 The 'tombstone' real light fitting was used on Harleys between 1948 and 1954.

071 On February 1 1994, Harley tried to copyright the sound of its engines. Several other manufacturers objected and the legal move was quietly dropped.

072 In February 2007, 2,700 Harley workers at the York, Pennsylvania plant went on strike over pay and health benefits. The strike lasted a fortnight.

073 Harley introduced the Panhead in 1948 and sold a very satisfying total of 31,163 bikes that year.

074 Millionaire magazine publisher Malcolm Forbes (who died in 1990) gave Elizabeth Taylor a Harley as a birthday present. The colour was Purple Passion.

075 It's thought that the first woman to ride a Harley was Janet Davidson – Arthur, William and Walter Davidson's aunt.

076 The shed in which the first ever Harley-Davidson was built measured ten feet by fifteen feet and was in the Davidson family's back yard.

077 The first Harley factory – which they moved into in 1906 – on Chestnut Street (later Juneau Avenue) in Milwaukee measured forty feet by sixty feet. The company is still based at that address (but the building is rather larger).

078 In 1970, Carl Rayborn rode a Harley-Davidson Sportster-based streamliner to a new American and International record of 265.492 mph.

079 In 2004, Jay Leno of The Tonight Show auctioned his Road King in aid of the Asian tsunami. It raised $810,000. He later auctioned another bike to help the victims of Hurricane Katrina, which raised $1,550,100.

080 American Machine and Foundry (AMF), which was founded in 1900 and bought Harley-Davidson in 1969, was famous for making bowling alley mechanisms.

081 The bike with the maddest letter sequence name is the 2006 FLHTCUSE (the Screamin' Eagle Ultra Classic Electra Glide), which looks like a bad Scrabble hand.

082 The 1903 machine put out around 3 bhp and was good for about 6 mph.

083 In 2008, anti-lock braking systems and cruise control were offered as factory options on all tourers.

084 The 1981 models were the last to bear the badges of both Harley-Davidson and AMF.

085 H-D has had a dealership in Dubai in the United Arab Emirates for eighteen years.

086 By 1920, Harleys were on sale in 67 countries worldwide.

087 Until 1911, Harleys were supplied with either 26-inch or 28-inch wheels. There was no extra charge for the larger wheels.

088 In a shameful abuse of the English language, Harley described their fully-floating seat on the 1912 model as 'Ful-Floteing'.

089 Harley offered its first sidecar in 1914. It cost $85 and was a single-seater, painted grey with black striping.

090 Leo Payne's Harley-Davidson Sportster – the Turnip Eater – was the first machine to exceed the 200 mph mark, back in 1957.

091 The Harley-Davidson Museum in the Menomonee River Valley opened on June 1 2006, with a floor area of 130,000 square feet. A soccer pitch, by comparison, measures 58,000 square feet.

092 In 1922, Englishman Alfred Rich Child became the company's sales rep in Africa, and then two years later he established the Koto Trading Company in Japan, which established the Harley-Davidson Motorcycle Sales Company of Japan. Alfred Rich Child was the managing director.

093 The VRSCA V-Rod, launched in 2002, put out 115 horsepower at 8,250 rpm from its all-new 60-degree V motor – making it then the most powerful Harley of all time. For 2009, the V-Rod Muscle takes that up to 125bhp.

094 The original hyphen used in the middle of Harley-Davidson is on display at The Smithsonian museum in Washington DC.***

095 Alex Bozmoski is the director of H-D's Noise, Vibration, and Harshness division, responsible for making sure that Harleys sound like Harleys should. A whole laboratory in Wauwatosa is devoted to the task.

096 In adverts placed in magazines in late 1912, H-D made great play of Frank Lightner hitting 68 mph on a stock Harley at Bakersfield the previous Thanksgiving Day. Damn fast for 1912, when a lot of people still hadn't travelled faster than the speed of a cantering horse.

097 Harley-Davidson Moscow can be found on Nizhnie Mnevniki Strett in the Russian capital.

098 One Joseph Harley – from whom Bill Harley was descended – arrived in South Carolina in the winter of 1696/1697 and was granted 200 acres of land in Colleton County the following March.

099 Willie G Davidson is a graduate of the University of Wisconsin, holding a degree in graphic art. He then studied at the Art Center College of Design in Pasadena, California.

100 Joe Petrali broke the land speed record on March 13 1937 on his Harley streamliner. He clocked 136.183 mph and the record held until 1948.

101 Between 1999 and 2007, Ford USA sold more than 60,000 of their Ford Harley-Davidson F-150 pickup trucks.

102 Kegel Harley-Davidson in Rockford, Illinois, is the oldest Harley dealership in the United States. It seems likely that the company had Harleys for sale as early as 1910. H-D was certainly buying fasteners from them before that.

103 Willie G Davidson is on record as saying that the styling cues for the 1988 Fat Boy came from Flash Gordon, Buck Rogers and Captain Video.

104 In 2001, Forbes magazines named Harley-Davidson Business Of The Year.

105 The tough-as-hell XR-1000 was only produced in 1983, and sold for what was then a very high price of $7,000.

* Not actually true

** Sorry, another fib

*** There I go again, just can't help it